•THE GUARDIAN SERIES•

# THE SILVER GLASS

• BOOK TWO •

*Janifer C. De Vos*

*Illustrations by*
*Gwendolyn Babbitt*

MULTNOMAH
Portland, Oregon 97266

Cover design by Bruce DeRoos
Edited by Deena Davis

THE SILVER GLASS
©1990 by Janifer C. De Vos
Published by Multnomah Press
10209 SE Division Street
Portland, Oregon 97266

Multnomah Press is a ministry of Multnomah School of the Bible,
8435 NE Glisan Street, Portland, Oregon 97220.

Printed in the United States of America.

**Library of Congress Cataloging-in-Publication Data**

De Vos, Janifer C.
    The silver glass / Janifer C. De Vos: illustrations by
Gwendolyn Babbitt
        p.    cm. — (The Guardian series ; bk. 2)
    Summary: Erin slips through a silver mirror and meets a
Spanish Jew who has escaped from the inquisition in Spain, but
is experiencing turbulent times under Henry VIII in sixteenth-
century England.
    ISBN 0-88070-410-1  (pbk.)
    [1. Space and time—Fiction.  2. Christian life—Fiction.]
I. Title. II. Series: De Vos, Janifer C. Guardian series ; bk. 2.
PZ7.D4995Si     1990
[Fic]—dc20                                          90-47098
                                                         CIP
                                                          AC

91 92 93 94 95 96 97 98 99 - 10 9 8 7 6 5 4 3 2 1

*Dedicated with love to my mom,
who has always
encouraged me to
"write it down!"*

# Floorplans for
# Antiques, Antiquities, Inc.

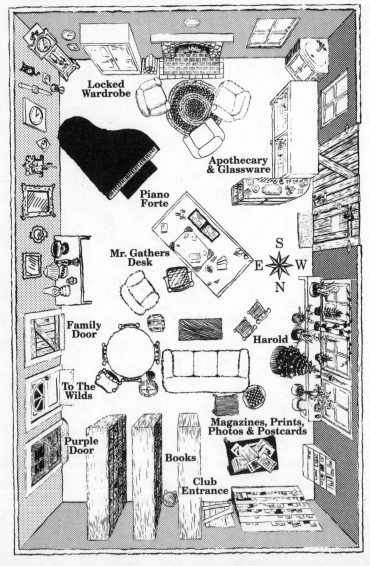

Locked Wardrobe

Apothecary & Glassware

Piano Forte

Mr. Gathers Desk

S
E W
N

Family Door

Harold

To The Wilds

Magazines, Prints, Photos & Postcards

Purple Door

Books

Club Entrance

Map illustration by Brian Ray Davis

# Contents

# *Prologue*

*"He needs to meet her soon," the dark-haired angel said to Sam. "He's ready to give up altogether."*

*"I know. But if she keeps reading from the book I gave her yesterday, she'll find it . . . maybe even today."*

*"And when she finds it? . . ."*

*"The mirrors will be delivered."*

*The two angels looked beyond where they were sitting into the quietness of the prayer chapel. One lone man knelt there, his forehead pressed against his hands. His loyal dog watched him from the sanctuary door.*

*"Help is coming," Sam whispered softly to the kneeling figure. "Don't give up."*

*The worshipper rose slowly, hugging his cloak about him, and walked stiffly out the arched doorway. The dog, tail wagging, followed him out into the snow.*

# 1
# At the Library

THE LIBRARY WAS almost deserted. Although most researchers and readers had already gone home, three young people sat at a table in one corner of the large, airy room. Several books were stacked in the center of the table.

Erin Grimly, long hair pulled back in the usual ponytail, was deeply engrossed in her reading. She and her friend Connie, who had just finished writing her tenth notecard, had gone to the library for several afternoons to work on a joint research project for their history class. Arnold, their long-time neighborhood friend, had joined them today under the guise of helping, but he really had teasing in mind.

"So, girls," Arnold said sarcastically, "have you discovered anything new and exciting about that great sailor, Christopher Columbus?" He sat down across from them and started restacking the column of books.

"Arn, leave those alone. We have them in the order we want them." Erin looked up only long enough to speak and then went back to her book. Connie ignored Arnold completely.

Not at all pleased with this lack of response, Arnold reached across the table and jerked Erin's book out of her hands.

"Hey! Stop it, Arnold!"

"Let's see, what have we here?" Arnold flipped the pages in mock interest. Clearing his throat loudly, he sat up in his chair. "'Christopher Columbus often took young boys on his voyages because of their willingness to work. The Admiral tired quickly of the complaining of the old salts on board.'" Then Arnold closed the book with a bang. Erin covered her eyes with one hand as she slumped in her seat. At least most other serious library users were already gone.

"Arn, give me the book, please." Erin spoke to him with a sigh. She had dealt with Arnold Lorenzo and his antics for so long that she knew enough not to encourage him with any show of irritation.

Instead of handing the book over, Arnold deliberately slid it across the table toward the tower of other books in the middle. The three children were startled by the quick intervention of a hand on the sliding book.

"We're getting ready to close, kids. Time to call it a day." Erin looked up with relief into the face of the new library assistant. He winked back at her.

"Okay, Sam. Could you save this book for

me?" Erin tapped the cover of the book Arnold had snatched.

"Sure, Erin. And . . . God go with you."

Erin looked up in surprise. Those were words she was used to hearing only inside Antiques, Antiquities, Inc., where she worked part-time after school. How would Sam know those words?

The girls gathered up their notebooks, index cards, and pencils. Arnold walked ahead, opened the glass double doors for them and then let go just as Connie and Erin came through.

"Ouch! Arnold Lorenzo! I am so sick of your juvenile behavior!" Connie shot an angry look at the boy. Arnold grinned wickedly and shoved his hands in his pockets. Jumping a low hedge, he disappeared around the side of the building.

"Well, at least we have a good start on our report. I think a couple more trips to the library—without Arnold—should give us all the information we need. What do you think, Erin?"

"A couple more trips should do it. But how will we manage to avoid Arnold?"

"Too bad we can't put him aboard a ship and send him far, far away . . . like to Alaska, or Siberia."

"Naw, I think too much of those poor people to send Arnold there!"

"Oh, I almost forgot. Erin, are you working

at A.A. Inc. on Saturday? I want to get my mom's birthday gift—I've had my eye on that ceramic angel on top of the apothecary cabinet. Do you think Mr. Gather would give me a break on the price?"

"Sure. I'll talk to him. See you later!"

Erin watched Connie walk away, and then her thoughts returned to the book she had been reading before Arnold so rudely interrupted. Ship life in 1492 had been quite an adventure.

The crunch of her gravel driveway brought Erin back to reality. A new thought of fig newtons and milk prompted her to run up the back steps, two at a time, into the kitchen.

Meanwhile, back in the library, Sam looked thoughtfully at the books Erin and Connie had left behind.

"She's on her way," he said to the empty room. "She found it this afternoon. Tell High Council to go ahead." And then Sam vanished.

# 2
# "Mirror, Mirror . . . "

ERIN HAD EXPECTED to find her mother in the kitchen, but instead she opened the back door to silence and found a note on the table. "Gone to have coffee with Mrs. Chloetilde. Will be home in time to cook dinner. Mr. S. was here. He has something new he wants you to see. Love, Mom."

*I wonder what's up?* Erin thought to herself.

She went out the back door toward the rock pile, walked over the little bridge and up the path to the old barn that was now an antique shop where she worked after school. The green enameled front door shone in the sunlight, as did the brass plate in the door's middle. Erin read the words printed there today.

*Snow White's wicked stepmother had one,*
*Your father couldn't shave without one,*
*You would be annoyed if you broke one,*
*Of what does Noah have more than one?*

"Hmmm. Now this is interesting. You usually let me in by giving me a little poem with a blank to fill in at the end." Erin looked questioningly at the green door. She watched to see if anything would change on or around the placard. Suddenly, the poem disappeared from the brass plate altogether and was replaced by one word: *Guess*.

"Come on, this isn't fair. Mr. Sebastian is waiting for me."

But the door was stubborn. The word remained on the brass plate, the shop door tightly closed. Well, what was there to guess? What was the unknown quantity in the riddle? That was easy—whatever "one" was.

"I guess that what Noah has more than one of is a mirror." Erin spoke firmly to the door and watched with relief as the placard gleamed gold, the words dissolved, and the door swung open, ringing the bell to herald her entrance.

"Hello! Hello! Is anybody home?" Erin took off her sweater and hung it on the hook by the front door. She looked approvingly at her surroundings and smiled at this place she had come to love. Antiques, Antiquities, Inc. was much more than an antique shop to her. It was a school of sorts where she was learning the most amazing things.

Erin stepped further into the large room, still unable to locate either Mr. Gather, the proprietor of the shop, or his junior partner, Mr. Noah Sebastian. Her eyes scanned the shop's contents: shelves of books of various shapes, sizes, and ages on the north wall; adventure doors for rent that opened into the most amazing places were in a row on the east wall alongside Mr. Gather's prized collection of antique clocks. Noah's piano forte rested in the corner. The ever-burning fireplace and three comfortable armchairs took up much of the south end of the room. Mr. Gather's apothecary section and collection of exotic and rare plants sat under the high west windows of the shop.

"Erin! Hello! Over here." The voice came from behind a large roll-top desk in the center of the room.

"Noah! What are you doing? I got a note from Mom that said you had something to show me. What is it?" Erin rounded the edge of the oak desk. Three wooden packing crates sat unopened on the floor. Noah Sebastian knelt next to the longest of the three, a crowbar in his hands.

"These were delivered this afternoon. I've been waiting for you to get here. I could use another pair of hands to help open them up."

"The front door just gave me a riddle about mirrors. Are these mirrors then?" Erin placed her hands where Noah pointed and gripped supportively as he gently inserted the bar into a corner of the crate and began loosening the slats. "It's coming, I can feel it." Erin slid her hands further into the wrappings and felt the shape of a wood frame.

"They're either mirrors or paintings. This is usually the way such things are packed for shipping or storage." Without warning the slats fell away, and Erin was left supporting a heavy, brown-paper parcel. She held on as Noah carefully pulled away the wrapping from a large oval mirror resting on a swivel base.

"It's lovely, Noah. How old do you think it is?"

"I haven't had much experience with mirrors, but I'm sure Mr. Gather will know something, or he'll at least know where we can find out more about it."

Erin stood back to get a full view of the mirror. It was smudged and fingerprinted around the edges. The wood was dull with a crusty brown dirt that spoke of years of neglect. She stooped to retrieve some of the brown wrapping, hoping for a clue to the mirror's origin or age, but was disappointed to find the paper blank and extremely gritty. A bulge near the edge of the paper on the floor caught her attention, and she bent to investigate. The bulge moved. She jumped back and started to laugh.

"Parenthesis, you dumb cat! Come out of there!"

A large white head appeared from under the wrapping. The bulge shifted sideways, and the head disappeared under the brown paper again as the cat continued her explorations.

"Well, Erin, there are two more to open. What do you say we get them unpacked first and then clean them up?"

Erin nodded, and they went to work unpacking the second crate. This one was more rectangular in shape, and Erin was able to pull the object out before Noah had loosened all the slats.

"Noah, where are you going to put these? Our wall space is pretty well taken up."

"Well, actually, I was hoping Mr. G. would let me have some of the wall space by his clocks."

"If you think Mr. Gather is going to give up one of his precious clock's hanging space for this, you are sadly mistaken!"

Noah smiled mischievously at Erin and set to work on the third crate. Of the three, it was the largest and most carefully packed, and it took all the strength Noah had to even insert the tip of the crowbar between the slats. Erin stood back and waited for a chance to slip her hands inside the crate and grasp the last mystery package.

"You know, Erin, this one feels a lot lighter than the other two. Maybe this is a painting." Noah pushed the tip of the crowbar in and widened the space he had already made. Without warning, the crowbar slipped, and the sound of breaking glass filled the shop. "Uh, I guess it was another mirror." Noah's shoulders sagged as he jerkily tried to remove the crowbar from the crate. The tip caught a slat on the way out, and the other slats sprang open as if on command. Erin grabbed frantically for the large parcel and caught it just in time.

"Well, I'm inclined to throw this one away."

"Let's at least unwrap it and see what the frame looks like. I can feel some kind of pattern through the paper."

Slowly, slowly, Noah pulled on the top edges of the frame, dislodging it from the rest of its packaging. Two-thirds of the mirror and all of the frame were intact. The four corners were ornately decorated with carved grape leaves that spilled over on the mirror surface. The glass itself had a silvery hue, and as Erin looked into it, she had a sensation of depth and movement that surprised and startled her.

"Man, I wish I hadn't broken this." Noah spoke in a voice heavy with remorse. "If only I'd been more careful."

# 3
# Mysteries

NOAH CAREFULLY RETRIEVED several pieces of glass from the bottom of the package. Then Erin carried it over to the desktop and gently tipped the packaging sideways to let any loose pieces slide out.

"Let's clean up the other mirrors first, and then we'll come back to this little problem and see what we can do."

When Erin returned from the apothecary shelves with her cleaning paraphernalia, Noah took a rag and a bottle of wood cleaner from her and began gently rubbing the frame around the swivel-based oval mirror. Erin copied his motions on the smaller rectangular frame resting against Mr. Gather's desk.

"These frames are really dirty. How long would you say they've been in storage, Noah?"

"It's hard to tell. You've cleaned this shop enough to know how dirty things can get in just a short time. But judging from the layers of caked-on gook, I'd say they've been put away at least fifty years, if not longer. This brown paper interests me, too. I've not felt a weight or texture of this kind before. I remember another time when you were using this ammonia stuff and got quite a surprise!" Noah said, laughing.

"You know," Erin said thoughtfully, "that seems like a long time ago. . . . "

"Erin, Noah, hello! What are you two so busily refurbishing?"

Erin knew the speaker was Mr. Gather, but his present location wasn't immediately evident. He wasn't coming through the front door. He wasn't sitting by the fireplace or coming through one of the adventure doors on the east wall of the shop . . . so Erin looked up. First, she saw brown leather shoes coming through the ceiling. Legs came after the shoes as if they were walking down stairs. And then, completely visible in mid air, she saw Mr. Gather. He stepped down to the ground-floor level and walked over to the other two workers. She knew she should be used to the unusual entrances and exits of her employers, but having someone come from a seemingly invisible second story left her with a strange sensation.

"Noah, what interesting pieces! Wherever did you find them?" Mr. Gather inspected the three mirrors approvingly. "These will make good additions to our stock."

"They were just delivered a little while ago . . . I assumed you knew they were coming." Noah looked questioningly at his senior partner.

"No, I know nothing about them."

"Have you seen anything *strange* in these yet, Erin?" Mr. Gather smiled in her direction.

"No!" said Erin. "But if I do see anything in these mirrors, I promise not to scream and run."

Erin vividly remembered her scare of several months before. She had been helping Mr. Gather clean the window panes on the adventure doors when a face appeared on the other side of the purple one and scared her badly. The face belonged to Demont, an angry boy who lived in the desert region behind the purple door. Demont had been seeking escape from there when Erin last encountered him. The purple door had remained locked from both sides ever since she had accidentally fallen through it.

"What do you suppose has happened to Demont?" Erin put her cleaning rag down and looked at Mr. Gather. "And I haven't seen Dr. Banushta since I left her behind the purple door. Will she ever be allowed to come back?"

"I've had only brief conversations with Protaimeus, Demont's guardian angel, since your adventure behind the door. He left me with little hope for Demont's recovery." Mr. Gather looked thoughtfully at Erin. "As for Dr. Banushta . . . she is back on earth, but will not be visiting here any time soon."

"Mr. G., where should we put these? Two of

them are almost ready for display, but I broke the third and . . . Erin, look at this!"

Erin looked at the spot where Noah was pointing. The third mirror leaned against Mr. Gather's desk, its glass mysteriously whole once more.

Erin looked questioningly at Mr. Gather. His face flashed sudden intuition that jolted him into action.

"Noah, Erin, I think High Council has its hand in all this. I want the two of you to continue your clean-up job on these mirrors. There may be a clue on one of them. I assume you both have already studied the wrappings in which they came?"

"Yes, Mr. G. I looked for some writing, numbers, something to give us an idea of the mirrors' origins. There wasn't anything."

"Except . . . " said Noah hesitatingly, "the paper didn't feel like the typical texture or weight of packing material. Oh, and Erin, we didn't look at the wood of the crates. Maybe the slats have been marked in some way."

They hurried around the desk to the pile of wooden slats scattered on the floor. As Erin bent down to pick up a slat it began to fade. She frantically grabbed at what swiftly became empty air. Looking around in disbelief she saw Noah having the same experience with an armload of boards he had managed to pick up.

"Well, so much for that plan." Noah grinned sheepishly at Erin. "I think Plan B was to clean these mirrors up and see what's under all the dirt. Right, Mr. Gather?"

This time their rubbing and scrubbing was done with vigor born of a curious excitement. "What are we looking for?" Erin asked Noah.

"Something that would mark these mirrors in such a way as to show they were High Council property, I guess." The energetic movements of Noah's hands were subtly matched by the strains of Baroque music floating through the air. Erin grinned. Where there was Noah, there was music. One of his many gifts was the ability to just think about music and have his brain waves become audible.

"Erin! I think I've found something. Come look at this."

He stood back so Erin could get a better view. In the lower corner of the frame the sign of infinity with a dove in the center had been painstakingly carved into the wood: the sign of High Council Guardians.

"Well, well," said Mr. Gather. "Let's sit down over a good strong cup of tea and discuss this."

Erin and Noah hurriedly collected their cleaning materials and stowed them under the apothecary sink. Having set the tea things out on a tray, Erin chose the black and gold tea tin containing Mr. Gather's favorite blend. They always had the black and gold when something special happened.

Mr. Gather removed the steaming kettle from the corner of the fireplace and poured the boiling water over the tea leaves that Erin had

spooned inside the china teapot. The three of them sat impatiently while the tea steeped the prescribed three to five minutes.

Erin looked out beyond the little circle of chairs. The large room reflected the warm yellow glow of the late afternoon sun. She heard the familiar ticking of the clocks on the wall, smelled the aromas of old books, old furniture, lemon oil, and the burning wood in the fireplace. She was acutely reminded of being part of two radically different worlds. One held her family and friends, her schoolwork, her social life, her everyday existence. The other had started in January when she walked through the door of Antiques, Antiquities, Inc. Here she had discovered the special place she was to take in the eternal scheme of things as a Guardian—a person who promises to love and serve the King with all his heart, mind, and soul, and to love his neighbor as himself. Mr. Gather, a Guardian himself, was her teacher, as were her experiences here in the shop and out in her world. She longed for the day when she would receive her Guardian ring, a token of high esteem from High Council.

Erin looked expectantly at the two men sitting opposite her, hoping as always for a more complete explanation of matters she did not understand. They smiled back in a noncommittal fashion that left Erin wondering, not for the first time, who they really were.

"How's your Christopher Columbus research coming along?"

"It's fascinating. Connie and I are learning a lot . . . oh, before I forget, Connie would like to buy that angel on top of the cabinet for her mom's birthday. I told her I'd talk to you about the price."

"No problem there. I'm delighted to have it go to a good home."

"Mr. Gather, what's the scoop on the mirrors? Do you have any ideas? Can we assume all three mirrors are from High Council? The symbol is only on the silver glass. How do we know what to do next?"

Mr. Gather looked over Erin's head into space. "We clean the mirrors, hang them, and wait."

Wait. Erin didn't want to wait. She looked at Mr. Gather, and her eyes fell on his Guardian ring. She got up the nerve to ask the question she'd wanted to ask for weeks.

"Mr. Gather, don't you think it's about time the Council awarded me my ring?"

He didn't answer, but his smile encouraged her to continue. "I've studied what I'm supposed to have studied, I've memorized everything you've asked me to memorize. I'm always where

I'm supposed to be when I'm supposed to be there. . . . " She was surprised at the level of frustration and impatience in her voice. Then she heard the sad strains of a cello solo fill the room. She looked accusingly at Noah.

Noah grinned mischievously back at her, and the music stopped.

Mr. Gather drank from his cup and waxed philosophical. "Receiving your ring and the second coming of the King are much alike. 'We know neither the day nor the hour'—Matthew 24:36." He gently tapped the cover of his Bible which always sat on the little table next to his chair.

Erin frowned. She tried to reason with herself. It was, after all, only a ring. But it symbolized more than that. It represented achievement, becoming, belonging, acceptance.

"Noah, aren't you tired of waiting?"

"Waiting?" asked Noah in feigned ignorance. "Waiting for what?"

"Your ring!" Erin said in exasperation. "You've waited much longer than I."

"Wrong!" said Noah with a triumphant twinkle in his eye. "I've not waited at all because I'm not a Guardian!"

"What? You're kidding! I just assumed that since Mr. Gather was, then you . . . I mean, what else?" Erin stopped herself just in time.

Noah laughingly finished her sentence for

her. "What else could I be? That's for me to know and you to figure out!"

Erin walked home that afternoon in a mental dither. Things were certainly not turning out as she had expected.

# 4
# Reconnaissance

THE LOGS ON the smoldering fire smoked and sizzled, sending a dim orange glow into the dark room. Parenthesis lay curled up, snug and warm in Erin's chair. All was quiet.

Suddenly Parenthesis turned over and opened one eye. A muffled sound was coming from the rear wall of the shop. Her sharp eyes focused quickly in the gloom and settled on the doors for rent. Jumping off the chair, she walked over to investigate. The steady rhythmic noise seemed to quicken, grow louder. Parenthesis walked slowly past each door: The Family Door, the Door to the Wilds, and finally the Purple Door. She sat down and waited as the door trembled. Then Parenthesis saw space grow between the door frame and the door itself. This had gone far enough. Time to sound an alarm.

Before Parenthesis had time to turn and summon help, the door burst open and rough hands grabbed the cat, stuffed her quickly into a burlap sack, and flung her back into the purple depths behind the now wide open door.

An unwelcome visitor stepped carefully into the room. Seeing no immediate threat to his

presence, he pulled the purple door almost closed. He walked past the other doors and stood in front of one of Noah's new mirrors. He smiled back at his curly-headed reflection and then sauntered to the chairs by the fire, choosing Mr. Gather's. Laughing into his hands, he leaned back and breathed deeply.

"Well, Demont, you've done it this time! To have gotten this far . . . to have gotten this far is certainly beyond our wildest dreams!" He put his dirty heels on the chair's beige cushion and wrapped long arms around his bony knees. "We're out, Demont. But are we ready to stay out, or do we want to go back now so that we can come again?" He gazed into the fire and seemed to lose himself in it. Then he slid one hand into his pocket and drew out a rectangular black panel which he lovingly caressed.

Suddenly he sat up, planted his feet on the braided rag rug, and thrust the panel deep in his pocket. "What happens if we can't get here again, though?" He sat back in the chair and held his knees. "But I'm not fully prepared. It's too soon, and I'm just not ready." His words came out more agitatedly. "I've got to go back. I just can't do it now. Later. Later." He jumped out of the chair, ran across the dark room, and in his haste bumped into the three-legged stool holding Noah's oval mirror. The stool and mirror teetered and fell with a resounding crash. Frantic with haste, he lost his sense of direction for a second and wasn't sure where the purple door was. By now Parenthesis had escaped from the sack and was howling on the other side of the door to get back into the shop. Rushing toward the sounds of her cries, the boy located the door, jerked it open, and shrieked as the enraged cat streaked past him. He went through the door and slammed it shut just as Mr. Gather hurried into the room with Noah close behind.

"Lights, please." He spoke authoritatively into the air.

On seeing the broken glass and the cat so close to the mess, he immediately assumed that Parenthesis had broken the mirror. He bent down to pick up the cat, scolding her gently.

"Parenthesis! I've told you before, no wild parties down here." The insulted cat struggled to get out of his arms.

Noah sadly examined the broken remains of the oval mirror. The glass had shattered into a thousand pieces. The frame had snapped off of its base, and the front rim was completely separated from the back.

"Mr. G., I'll clean this up now, if you like."

"That really isn't necessary, Noah. This can wait until morning." Parenthesis succeeded in wriggling free from Mr. Gather and made a mad dash for the purple door. She hissed and spat at it.

"Well, what do you suppose that is all about?"

Mr. Gather started to reply, when something on the floor in front of the purple door caught his eye.

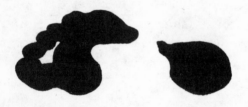

"Noah, look at this." There on the hardwood floor was the dusty print of a bare foot. "When did you last mop the floors on this side of the shop?"

"This afternoon I wet-mopped this part of the floor because Erin told me there seemed to be a lot of dust back here. Are you thinking what I'm thinking?"

The two looked at each other and then toward the purple door.

"I'll stay down here and clean up. Surely our visitor won't be back again tonight."

Mr. Gather didn't look altogether convinced. "I wonder . . ." he said softly to himself. "Well, I'll leave the cleaning to you. I'm sorry about the mirror."

The older gentleman turned away and disappeared from the ground floor of the shop. With a resigned smile, Noah filled the room with energetic music and picked up the broom. He carefully swept up all the bits of glass and wood, filling a small garbage can with the remains. He decided to mop the floor around the doors next and went to get the mop.

"Come on, Noah, you just used the thing. Where did you put it?" he mumbled under his breath. Then he remembered that he had left the mop and bucket behind the last bookshelf only this afternoon when his cleaning had been interrupted by a customer. He was bending over to grasp the bucket's handle when he heard Parenthesis growl. Turning just in time to see the purple door open a crack, he hid himself behind the bookshelves. He could see the door without being seen . . . he hoped.

Slowly, slowly, the door opened. A boy about Arnold's age stepped into the room. He looked all around with shrewd eyes. Black, curly hair framed his pale face. The boy wore a loose fitting shirt and baggy pants held up by a length of woven hemp. He quietly closed the purple door with both hands. Stepping further into the room, he hesitated only a moment and then went straight to Mr. Gather's chair.

# 5
# Fire!

"WELL, DEMONT, HERE you are again. I wonder what time it is?" He looked at the clocks on the wall.

Noah edged closer to the end of the bookshelf so he could see better. His hand bumped a row of volumes, causing them to teeter precariously. He caught them just in time.

Demont looked into the fireplace, now filled only with glowing embers. He sat back in the chair and laughed outright.

"We're out! We're out!" He looked sharply around the shop. "But I wonder . . . is it still the night of the broken mirror, or is that night long past? Who can say? Who will tell me?" Getting up, he stood before the fireplace, warming his hands.

"We're out, and this time we're staying out!" he said defiantly. "No one is going to make me go back. No one!" He spoke more like a naughty five-year-old than the almost teenager Noah guessed him to be. He reached for one of the long matches on the hearth and stuck the matchhead into an ember. It sparked and hissed. Demont was fascinated by the flickering flame. He moved toward the center of the shop, watching the matchstick burn.

"Protaimeus must not take me back. But how can I stop him from coming to get me?" Demont talked to the rapidly shortening matchstick. "I know . . . I know a way to stop him. If there is no door, he cannot come. So . . . I will burn the purple door, and that will be the end of that!"

Demont threw the match into the fire just as it was about to burn him. Glancing around the room, he saw what he wanted: a few rags and a bottle of cleaning fluid.

Noah decided this was definitely the time to intervene. He walked softly from his hiding place and stood between Demont and the doors on the east wall.

Demont grabbed the rags and fluid, spun around, and stopped dead in his tracks.

"Where did you come from?" He snarled. He whisked the rags and bottle behind his back.

"Hello. May I help you?"

"Where did you come from?" Demont persisted angrily.

"I live here. This is my home and my work place. And you?" Noah spoke gently and took a step toward the boy.

"Stop! Stay away from me!" Demont turned in panic.

"I'm not going to hurt you. No one here will. Why don't you sit by the fire and have a cup of tea with me? Maybe I can help you in some way."

"Oh, right," Demont said sarcastically. "You sound very much like Protaimeus." Quite without warning he changed his attitude. "Okay. I'll have tea with you. You're right. Maybe you can help me in some way." He looked sideways at Noah, who watched him closely.

"Fine. Just relax, and I'll have tea for us both in a minute." Noah walked slowly toward the apothecary to retrieve the tea things, never taking his eyes off Demont. Demont slid into the chair closest to the fireplace with his back to Noah.

"So, tell me, what's your name? Where are you from?" Noah talked as he arranged the cups, saucers, and spoons on the tray. He reached for the tea tin and the china teapot.

"Oh, around," said Demont noncommittally.

"I think you've been here before . . . here in the shop." Noah let his words sink in. "Is that possible?"

Demont didn't answer.

"I think your name is Demont, and you know a friend of mine . . . Erin Grimly."

Demont sat up in his chair. "What? You know the girl-sneak?" He said the words before thinking and immediately slapped his hand over his mouth. He became agitated, rocking back and forth in the chair, his arms folded across his chest, mumbling things under his breath.

Noah brought the tea tray over and set it on the end table. "Just let me pour the water on the tea leaves and we'll be ready." Outwardly, Noah appeared calm. Inwardly, he was watching Demont's agitation with growing concern.

Noah reached past Demont to pull the kettle out from over the coals where Mr. Gather always kept it simmering, ready at any given time for a cup of tea. As he used both hands to lift the kettle off its metal hook, Demont made his move.

He splashed a rag with cleaning fluid and touched a corner of it to the coals in the fireplace. It burst into flame.

"Demont! No!"

Demont ran toward the purple door, bottle of fluid and flaming rag in hand. Noah set down the steaming kettle and ran after him.

Still several feet away from the purple door, Demont threw the bottle, fluid splashing against the door frame. He tossed the flaming rag into the puddle of strong-smelling stuff. The blaze was instantaneous.

Noah grabbed the mop near the door and began beating out the flames. Mr. Gather was suddenly beside him, pouring dirt from a large flowerpot onto the fire. The flames sputtered out as quickly as they had begun. Both men looked away from the now smoldering wreckage of the purple door and turned to Demont, who was enraged by what they had done.

"You've ruined everything! Why did you have to put it out?" He ran behind the glassware. "I'm not going back there. I'll never go back there." He toppled one case and the sound of breaking glass filled the shop.

Noah signaled "separate and circle" with his hands to Mr. Gather, who walked slowly toward the fireplace in full view of Demont. Noah walked behind the tables, chairs, and lamps and halted in front of Harold, the omnivorous conifer. He could see Demont standing by the fireplace.

"Come on, son. Let's sit down and talk this out." Mr. Gather's tone was soothing and even.

"No! Stay away from me!"

Mr. Gather sat down in his chair. Noah walked softly past the front door and stood motionless at the end of the now toppled glassware shelf. He could hear Demont's heavy breathing. It was only a matter of time now. Demont was not going anywhere. Noah relaxed and that was his mistake.

With a sudden burst of energy, Demont charged back to the shop's adventure doors and pulled frantically at the doorknobs. Noah moved swiftly to pin him in a corner, but Demont was now standing in front of the silver glass hanging between the doors and the clocks. Angrily, he raised his fists to smash the mirror's surface. Noah sprinted forward to grab Demont's hands, partly out of concern for the boy, and partly out of concern for his mirror. But Demont was too fast. He swung his fists into the silver glass with all his might.

Noah blinked. He expected to hear shattering glass followed by Demont's screams of pain. He heard neither. The room was silent. It was also empty of one young man named Demont.

"Noah, I think we have a problem," Mr. Gather said with surprising calm.

Wordlessly, Noah walked over to the mirror and saw his reflection in the glass. He tentatively reached out to touch the silver surface and was astonished to discover that the glass swallowed his hand up to his wrist. He pulled it out again as if he had been burned. He then extended both hands to touch the glass. They disappeared into the silver up to his wrists and then his elbows when he extended them farther.

He pulled his arms out again and gave a low whistle. "Where do you suppose my hands are when they are on the other side of this glass?" Noah turned and looked inquiringly at his partner.

"I don't know, Noah. But where your hands go, there goes Demont."

Noah stuck a hand in the mirror again. This time he let it go in clear up to his shoulder. He felt a kind of tugging, sucking sensation, as if a vacuum cleaner were pulling him into the glass. With some effort, he pulled his arm back out again.

"I guess there's no chance good ol' Demont will come back by himself?" Noah looked over at Mr. Gather.

"I doubt it," he replied. "We'll have to bring him back."

# 6
# Through a Glass Darkly

ERIN TOOK HER time walking up the sloping hill of her back yard. She was enjoying the delicious feeling of no pressure to do much of anything on this bright Saturday morning. She had finished her schoolwork Friday night while babysitting the Ring twins, and her piano lesson wasn't for hours. She wasn't expected at Antiques, Antiquities, Inc. until early afternoon. Still, she felt mysteriously compelled to cross the fence and go to the shop.

The strong smell of burned wood hung in the air, different from the usual fresh spicy smell of the shop's fireplace. Before Erin reached the door, it opened and Noah huffed out, carrying a bulky garbage bag.

"Good morning!" Erin said cheerfully. "What's the awful burned wood smell?" She sniffed the air distastefully.

"Good morning, yourself," said Noah with a smile. He put the garbage bag down. "We had a visitor last night."

"Oh?" Erin looked at Noah and then realized the meaning behind his words. "Well, don't just stand there—tell me about this!"

Noah kept smiling and walked away from Erin toward the garbage cans around the side of the barn. He returned quickly, clapping his hands together to clean off some of the dust and dirt. "Who was the last person to call you 'girl-sneak?'"

Erin stared at him in astonishment. "You mean to tell me that Demont was here, in the shop, last night?"

"Yes, he was. Come on in, Mr. Gather is waiting for us."

The pungent smell was even stronger inside the shop. Mr. Gather closed the ledger in front of him, sat back in his chair, and looked at them with serious eyes.

"It's time for a staff meeting, I think. Erin, I assume Noah has told you we had a visitor last night?"

Erin nodded. They all sat down by the fireplace, and Erin looked expectantly at Mr. Gather.

She sniffed the air again and made a face. "That smell almost makes me sick to my stomach. Where was the fire?"

"Take a look at the purple door," said Noah softly.

Erin sat forward in her chair a little and gasped. The northeast corner of the shop was covered with a charcoal blackness. The burned doorframe had rippled and buckled from the searing heat.

"Demont didn't want Protaimeus to come after him, so he tried to burn the purple door," said Noah.

"I'd say he almost succeeded," said Erin under her breath. "So where is Demont now? Have you got him locked up somewhere? Did Protaimeus come and get him?" She settled back in her chair, sure of a positive answer.

Noah looked at Mr. Gather, and Mr. Gather looked at Noah.

"You have him upstairs, right?" Erin asked with growing curiosity. "Uh-oh," she said softly when her question went unanswered.

Noah got up. "Come with me. I have something else to show you." He walked to the mirror hanging on the wall next to Mr. Gather's collection of antique clocks. He held his hand in front of Erin and the mirror. "Now you see it," he said, thrusting his hand through the glass, "and now you don't!" His hand disappeared up to the elbow.

"Wow!" was all Erin could say. She stepped closer to Noah and tentatively touched her finger to the surface of the glass. It disappeared up to the first knuckle. "What in the world? . . ."

Noah had pulled his arm back out again and looked at Erin. "That, to answer your earlier question, is where Demont has gone. We don't know where or to what the mirror might lead; we only know that Demont went through it late last night and has not returned."

Erin looked at her reflection. The shop's images mirrored back to her were ones she knew well, and yet, there was an indefinable quality, a depth in the reflection that she did not understand.

"How are you going to get him to come back?" Erin asked them suddenly. "Does it matter if he stays there?"

"That's what we need to discuss. I, for one, feel a strong responsibility toward negotiating Demont's safe return to the region behind the purple door. He is a seriously disturbed young man. This mirror's environment might not hold sanctuary for him."

"Do we know anything about what's on the other side?" asked Erin.

"Only that it has purpose for us, because of the sign on the corner of the frame. I feel it is safe for us to travel through the mirror because the King's sign is on it."

"Oh, boy," said Erin, beginning to feel a sense of dread.

"We need to move on this immediately. We have no idea how time on the other side of the mirror works, but after our experiences with the doors, we know that anything is possible."

"Well, Mr. G., I feel a certain sense of responsibility since I wasn't able to stop Demont from going through the mirror. I volunteer to go after him." Noah's words were sincere, but a bit lacking in enthusiasm.

"And, you know Mr. Gather, I should go, too, because I am the only one who knows Demont. I understand how he thinks . . . sort of. . . ." Erin stopped, remembering her previous experience with Demont.

Mr. Gather nodded. "I agree. You two are well-suited for this adventure. Erin, if you are gone overly long, I will assure your parents of your safety. As a matter of fact, I think I'll talk to them now."

Something in the way he spoke made Erin feel cold and not a little afraid. She bowed her head and was surprised to hear Mr. Gather praying beside her.

"Most gracious King, I ask your special blessing on these two servants as they go after one of Your broken ones. Grant them wisdom and safety. May Your purpose be achieved. Amen."

The three stood up and walked over to the mirror.

"Okay, Erin. I'll go first. Just be sure you come right after me. We definitely want to land in the same place at the same time." Noah put

out his arms as though he were about to execute a dive off a diving board. With a light spring, he went through the mirror and out of their sight.

"Bye, Mr. Gather."

"God go with you, Erin."

Erin followed Noah's example, even closing her eyes and holding her breath. As the tips of her outstretched fingers touched the glass, she bent her knees and leaped forward, leaving the security of the shop to enter . . . what?

# 7
# Face to Face

A STRONG VACUUM force pulled Erin through the glass to the other side. She fell a short distance to a rough-hewn stone floor. The landing hurt but was over so fast she hardly had time to think about it. The place was dark.

"Where are we?" Erin took Noah's proffered hand and stood up. Her words echoed around her. As her eyes grew accustomed to the dimness, she saw that she and Noah were in a back corner of a high-ceilinged room with walls of stone. "This place looks like a room in a castle . . . or a church." She whispered, and still her words bounced through the air. She turned around to see where they had entered, and then grabbed Noah's arm in panic.

"Noah, there's no mirror on this side!"

He turned and looked at the bare stone wall behind them, lifting one eyebrow. "Oh, my. This could be interesting. I'm just realizing that we forgot to ask Mr. Gather. . . ." he looked at Erin.

"How to get back. . . ." Erin finished the sentence for him. "Maybe that's why Demont didn't come back."

"Well, we can't worry about that now. We're

here, and we have a job to do."

They looked carefully at their new surroundings. Erin could see several rows of wooden benches in front of her and a set of steps leading up to a simple stone altar. The wooden pulpit put the whole room in its proper perspective.

"We seem to have landed in a church. Anglo-Saxon, I would say, judging from the architecture." Noah stepped into the aisle. Suddenly he put a warning finger to his lips. Following the direction of his gaze, Erin saw several reverently bowed heads in the front row.

"Noah," Erin whispered, "we're not dressed for this century . . . whichever one it is. Look what that lady is wearing!" New panic swept over her as she looked down at her bluejeans and knit jacket. The woman kneeling in the pew several rows ahead of them wore a long skirt and matching dark blouse with a shawl pulled tightly around her stooped shoulders.

"This could be a problem." Noah said thoughtfully. His voice sounded distracted. Erin looked at her companion.

"Noah, what—"

Erin was interrupted by the sound of advancing feet. Noah's strong arms suddenly pulled her aside. A choir of six or seven young boys walked down the aisle past her and filled the choir boxes in the middle of the sanctuary.

The sweet, clear sounds of voices singing the King's praises flowed through the air. Erin grinned as she heard Noah humming the tenor part.

When the singing was over, Noah whispered, "It must be evening. That was a chant for Evensong."

Erin looked at her watch—10:37. Well, that certainly wasn't right. As she picked up a small leatherbound book in the seat beside her, movement by one of the doors caught her eye. She strained to see. The form was familiar.

"Noah!" she hissed. "There's Demont! By the door! Quick! He's getting away!"

They ran across the floor after the fleeing figure who dashed out the heavy wooden church door into the twilight. Noah had sprinted ahead of Erin and saw their quarry dash around the side of the church. As Noah turned the corner, he saw Demont collide with the parish priest.

"Please, please, sir. They are after me. They'll catch me and send me back! Sanctuary! Sanctuary!" Demont clung to the man's vestments and fell to his knees.

The priest looked over the boy's head in the direction of Noah and Erin. He put a supportive hand on Demont's shoulder. "Arise, my son. I see but one pursuer, and that one seems too fair of

face to be of harm to you." He pulled Demont to his feet and called out to Erin. "Come hither, child, so I can better see you."

The evening had truly come upon them now. Erin could feel a rising wind and a chill that bit to her bones. Knowing Noah was right beside her, she stepped confidently forward. She watched Demont flinch continually under the cleric's grasp. She remembered his violent reaction when she had once accidentally touched him. She could only guess as to the amount of pain Demont was enduring now.

"Good evening," she said in her most confident tone.

Demont stood shaking beside the priest. "Don't let them take me back, please! I hate it there."

"Them? I see but a young lad—or is it a girl in lad's clothing?" he said frowning and squinting. "Come forward and state your business."

Erin came forward with Noah beside her.

"We've come to help the boy . . . to take him home. He's not well," Noah said.

"Well, speak up, child. State your business." The priest grew increasingly impatient, acting as though Noah had not even spoken.

Erin looked at Noah and then at the man in front of her.

"We've come to take this boy home," Erin said, repeating Noah's words.

"*We?*" the priest questioned. "Are you not alone then?" He stepped closer to Erin, peering into the night around her. He gasped suddenly. "There! Behind you! I saw a shadow . . . your familiar spirit, girl?" He glared at her accusingly. "Is this the 'we' you speak of?" He pulled Demont to him as though to protect him. "And where is home?" he continued suspiciously.

Noah whispered softly in Erin's ear. "Come on, Erin. Let's go. We can keep an eye on Demont and get him when he's alone."

Demont let out a shriek. "They're going to

come after me later! I hear them talking." He tried to pull away from the older man but was held tightly. His face contorted in pain and a moan escaped him.

"You're bewitched, boy. Has this mistress cast a spell on you?"

Demont struggled all the more.

"Let me go! Don't touch me! You're hurting me!"

With a sudden burst of energy, Demont wrenched free of his captor and dashed away down the rutted, muddy road.

"Oh, no!" Erin leaped after him. Darkness hung heavily around them, punctuated here and there by the firelight spilling from cottages along the road's edge. Erin ran hard after Demont. The priest limped along after Erin, his robes billowing about his short legs.

# 8
# The Chase

THE FROZEN MUD ruts in the road made Erin's progress difficult, although Demont seemed to sail across the track with little trouble. He turned at the first possible opportunity and disappeared from view.

"Turn here, Erin!" yelled Noah. He sprinted past her and shot ahead around the corner.

They were just gaining on Demont when he took a detour through a chicken coop. He dashed through the low door with Erin and Noah right behind him. Hens squawked in rage. Feathers flew. Erin put up her hands to ward off the crazily flying birds. Fortunately, they were all outside again before too much damage was done.

Ahead of them a small cottage sat in the snow, and Erin could make out a line of trees behind it. She caught up with Noah, putting her hands on her knees, huffing to catch her breath. She stood up, pulling feathers out of her hair, and pushed her glasses back up on her nose.

"Let's duck behind this place so that we are out of sight of our priest friend," said Noah.

After moving quickly behind the cottage, Erin was able to see the trees and beyond. The ground sloped down to a partially frozen pond: a slushy mess with a liquidy hole in the center. Erin shivered as the warmth she had felt from the exertion of the chase dissipated.

"Do you see Demont?" Erin squinted into the dusk.

"No, but I hear him. Listen." Noah nodded in the direction of the line of trees and the pond.

At first Erin only heard the low creak of wind in frozen branches over her head. But then she heard the sound of feet trying to move quietly through crunching snow.

Noah spoke softly, "Erin, you like dogs, don't you?"

"Yes," she said, mystified as to why he would bring up dogs at a time like this.

"Well, there's one behind us who doesn't like us. Would you like to convince him we're friendly, or shall I?"

Erin turned to get a better look at the dog. At first she didn't even see it. Then, when it growled and showed its teeth, she saw its menacing outline against the chicken coop.

"Uh, you go right ahead." Erin swallowed hard as the dog advanced slowly toward them, his growl louder, his lips pulled back to reveal sharp teeth.

Noah walked slowly into the open, palms out and raised toward the dog. Erin heard a Strauss waltz.

"Sit, Sampson."

To Erin's astonishment, the dog sat down obediently on his haunches, mouth suddenly shaped into a grin. His tail wagged vigorously in time to the music, swishing snow back and forth on the ground.

Noah patted the dog on the head. "Good dog, good Sampson." After one last scratch under the dog's chin, Noah sent him on his way. Still in a state of disbelief, Erin watched as Sampson trotted around the side of the chicken coup and disappeared from sight.

"How did you do that?"

"Sampson just needed a little music. Now where has Demont gone?"

They looked toward the trees again, straining for some sight or sound of the boy.

Erin looked toward the pond. "Noah! There he is! Right by the ice!"

They hurried to the edge of the trees. The snowcovered ground in front of them had been broken by only one set of footprints.

"I can't tell where the ground ends and the pond begins," said Erin with concern. "I don't know if it's even safe to walk beyond here."

"Well, Demont's footprints are there to guide us part of the way, . . . I think it's time for a confrontation."

They walked out of the woods and onto the

slope leading down to the icy pond. Demont heard footsteps and whipped around to face them.

"I won't go back!"

"Demont, just listen a minute, please. " Erin yelled into the rising wind. She stepped into three or four more of Demont's footprints, coming within a few feet of the boy.

"No! Stay away from me. . . . Stay away!" Demont looked frantically behind Erin, and seeing Noah, he decided the only way to go was across the ice.

"Demont! No! The ice isn't safe . . ." Noah yelled.

Just then, the priest came to the top of the hill. "You there, boy! Stop, I say!"

Demont was frightened and confused. He turned back toward Erin and Noah, and then, on hearing the priest yell again, he stepped out toward the center of the pond. Erin heard the sickening sound of cracking ice.

"Erin, lie down right here on the ice," Noah commanded. "Demont," he yelled, "the ice around you is breaking up. You must listen to me."

The boy looked at Noah and stopped.

"Okay, Demont, I want you to very slowly sit down right where you are. Good. Now, Erin and I are going to reach out and get you and pull you back in. Okay, Erin . . . I'll hold your ankles, and you push yourself forward and grab Demont's wrists. Then I'll pull you both back."

"Noah, there's just one thing wrong with this plan."

"What?"

"Demont won't let me touch him. He won't let anyone touch him."

"Well, I don't see that we have any other choice, do we?"

"No, I guess not." Erin stretched out on the ice and began pulling herself forward. She felt Noah's firm grip on her ankles.

"Demont, reach for Erin's hands as soon as she's close."

Demont looked fearfully at Erin. "No! I won't touch the hands of Erin-sneak! It will hurt!" He started to move farther away from Erin, and they all heard the moan of over-stressed ice.

"Demont, grab my jacket sleeves. You don't even have to touch my hands; or I'll grab your cuffs and pull. Just don't go any farther away from me." Erin's arm muscles burned. "I wish we could call 911," she muttered under her breath.

The priest was watching everything from the hilltop.

"Okay, Demont, reach for Erin's sleeves," commanded Noah. "Erin, don't go any farther."

It took all the self-control Erin had to keep from grabbing Demont's wrists and jerking him

back with her onto the safer surface. She pulled her hands deep into her sleeves and offered Demont the empty cuffs. He grabbed them and held on gingerly.

"Okay, Noah. We've made contact. Pull away."

Erin felt herself moving backwards on the ice. Her knit jacket sleeves stretched, but Demont was moving in the same direction she was. The ice hissed and cracked but didn't break.

Demont suddenly released his grip on Erin's sleeves and rolled past her on the ice. He was up on his feet in a flash and ran up the slope past the priest and into the woods again.

Erin and Noah scrambled to the pond's edge, up the slope, and into the woods after Demont.

The priest limped after them, talking to himself, "She must be a witch! To have moved back and forth without falling through the ice like that is not natural!" With sudden zeal and ferocity he shook his stick in the air and started his chasing again, yelling "Witch! Witch!"

# 9
# Trapped!

DEMONT LEFT THE muddy track and crossed into a large yard with a hut at one end. He ran through the open door of the hut, not even glancing behind him. Erin ran after him.

"No, Erin, wait!" Noah called out behind her.

Without heeding his warning, she dashed through the door after Demont. The shelter was dark, and she stopped to let her eyes adjust. There was a loud scraping and scurrying to her left, and she turned to see Demont leap out a low window. She hurried over to the opening only to have shutters slammed in her face. Whirling around, she ran back to the front door to find it firmly shut. She ran back to the shutters and beat her fists against them to no avail. Then she threw her weight against the door and fell back into the center of the room onto the dirt floor.

"Noah?" she whispered hopefully. "Are you here?" The answering silence fed her rising fear.

She got up and beat against the door. "Let me out! Let me out!" She put her ear to the door, hoping to hear something. Several minutes passed. She could only make out the muffled sounds of several people talking, but their words were indistinct.

The unexpected hand on her shoulder frightened her so badly that she turned around punching wildly to ward off her attacker.

"Hey, this is no way to treat the rescue party!" Noah laughed.

"Noah, you scared me to death! How did you get in here? Now what are we supposed to do?" Erin shivered, hugging herself to get warm.

Noah looked around the sparsely furnished room. He could just make out a pile of straw in one corner, a small table with an unlit lantern setting on it, and a roughly made wooden chair beside it. Above the chair there was a row of pegs set in the wall. Noah walked over to the pegs and pulled down a cloak hanging there and wrapped it around Erin.

"Better?"

"Yes," Erin said gratefully. "It's kind of scratchy, but I can take it if it will keep me warm. But, Noah, aren't you cold? You have on a short-sleeved shirt."

"I'm fine. Now, Erin, you must listen to me and follow my directions exactly. There is a guard outside who means to keep you here. It seems that our priest friend thinks you may be a witch."

"That's ridiculous! What have I done to make

**70**

him think that?" Erin looked at Noah incredulously. "All we did was talk to him about taking Demont home. . . ." She stopped short. "Noah, why did he ignore you?"

"He didn't see me."

"But you were standing right next to me. How could he not see you?" Erin felt annoyed and confused. The room was growing colder by the minute. She shivered in spite of the warm cloak.

"Erin, I'm going to do some reconnoitering. I'll be back for you soon."

"Noah! Don't leave me here! And how do you plan to get out?"

"I'll get out the same way I came in. I'll be back. Don't worry. Just think warm thoughts."

"Noah, please take me with . . . Noah? Noah!" She jumped out of her chair and ran around the little room. Noah was gone.

Tears brimmed in Erin's eyes and anger mixed with fear burned in her chest. Why had he left her here? She stomped back to her chair and sat down.

The wind was picking up outside. She could hear it howl around the corners as she sat in almost total darkness. Looking at the lamp, she wondered if there were some matches around. Then she wondered if matches had been invented yet. She suddenly remembered the matches in her jacket pocket from her last Girl Scout camp-out. Lifting the glass globe of the lantern, she adjusted the wick and struck the match. It flared in welcome brightness. Fortunately, there was oil in the lamp; so when she touched the match to the wick, it burned merrily.

# 10
# Witches
# Are for Burning

ERIN HUDDLED IN the chair, cold, hungry, and tired. She looked around the small room, hoping to find something in addition to the cloak to keep her warm. The hut's walls were bare as was the dirt floor, except for the straw piled in one corner. The damp crept through Erin's clothing, chilling her to the bone. She stood up and started to pace in the little room.

"Noah, where are you?" she asked aloud.

Much to her surprise, there was a noise by the door. She stepped toward it and was greeted by a blast of frigid air and snowflakes.

"Noah?"

"Stand back, girl! Back to the chair," a gruff voice spoke into the room.

Erin obediently backed toward the chair. A young girl whom Erin guessed to be almost her own age stepped over the threshold with a basket and jug in her hands. Her blond hair was stuffed untidily into a small cap on top of her head. Her skirts brushed the floor as she walked to the table and put the basket and jug down. The man entering behind her carried a lantern and looked momentarily taken aback when he saw the lantern on the table was lit. He stepped back out into the snow.

"This is for you," the girl said softly. "The holy father didn't want you to starve before . . . before . . . well, you know." She looked away from Erin and turned to leave.

"No, wait, please. Stay and talk to me. I don't understand what you mean. Before what?"

"Come on, girl." The rough voice roared into the room. You've other serving to do tonight before your work is through."

Erin looked beseechingly at the other girl. "Can't you stay just long enough to let me eat? Then you could take the basket and jug back when I'm done. It would save you an extra trip."

The servant girl paused for a few seconds, her brow wrinkled with the effort of her thinking. "Yes, I will ask," she said with sudden resolution.

She disappeared out the door to speak with her gruff companion. Erin lifted the cloth covering the contents of the basket and saw generous slabs of bread and cheese resting next to an apple. She turned as she heard the door close and the crossbar slide into place. There stood the other girl, half hidden in the shadows cast by the flickering lamp.

"You must eat. My time with you will be

short. John has disobeyed the priest by letting me stay." The girl stepped farther into the room. "Are you really a witch?" she asked in a hushed voice. "John says you must be if you lit the lantern."

"No, I am most certainly not," said Erin. "And I can explain about the lantern. I lit it very scientifically—no witchcraft! But I am hungry. May I eat now?" The girl nodded, and Erin eagerly reached for the bread and cheese after putting the apple in her jacket pocket. It slid in with a little difficulty as there was something else sharing the small space.

Erin bowed her head to say a silent thank you to the Lord for providing for her needs and to ask for guidance and help for Noah, wherever he was.

When she opened her eyes, she saw the other girl looking at her with astonishment.

"To whom do you pray?" she asked accusingly.

"Why, the Lord, of course." Erin bit into a piece of bread and cheese. It tasted wonderful. She chewed, swallowed, and took another bite. "Is that water?" she pointed to the jug beside the basket.

"Yes, but I've forgotten to bring you a cup, so you'll have to drink from the jug."

"That's all right." Erin took the jug in both hands and lifted it to her lips. She was just about to take a drink when something in the back of her mind came to the front. Maybe she shouldn't be eating and drinking in this place. After all, she didn't even know where she was. She put the jug back down again. Since she had already swallowed some bread and cheese, and it certainly tasted like it was okay, she decided she'd keep eating that. She planned to save the apple for Noah.

"My name is Erin. What's yours?" she asked the girl between bites.

"I'll not be telling you my name. Witches should never know your true name," the girl said with a superior air. "And to what Lord do you pray? Is it the familiar spirit the priest saw with you on the road yonder?" The servant girl walked over to the heap of straw in the corner of the room and sat down on it. She pulled her cloak around her shoulders and tucked it under her feet. She didn't seem to feel the cold as Erin did.

Erin could feel the other girl's judgmental gaze on her white knit jacket, bluejeans, and tennis shoes.

"If you won't tell me your name, then tell me some things about this place. What is it called? Where am I exactly?"

"Why, you're in England, of course. Just outside London." She looked at Erin quizzically. "Did you perhaps lose your way while flying on your broomstick?"

Erin chose to ignore the question. "What year is it?"

"Well, I'm not sure about that. I know we are in the 1530s. Which year exactly I don't know."

"The 1530s! Wow! I never would have guessed that." Erin said under her breath.

"I'd better be going before the mistress looks for me." The girl reached for the basket as she rose to leave.

"Please stay a few more minutes and talk to me," Erin pleaded. "I'm not a witch, and I'm certainly not in any position to hurt you. I'd like to know more about this place and time." Erin felt the apple in her pocket. "Here, you can have my apple if you'll stay." She pulled the apple out of her pocket and another object came out with it and fell to the floor. The other girl snatched it up before Erin could retrieve it.

"Why do you have this, witch-girl? I have seen this book in the hands of the priest at services. It is a holy book, a church book." Her face suddenly filled with fear. "Now I have touched it. I'll be punished surely." She started sobbing. "I'll never get to heaven, never! I am always doing something wrong. I will never be good enough! Ellsbeth," she said to herself, "you are doomed." Her hands fell hopelessly to her sides, and she turned to go.

"Ellsbeth. Is that your name?"

The other girl nodded.

"Ellsbeth, none of us is good enough to go to heaven. But in the Bible it says we are saved by faith in Jesus, not by the good things we do. It's a gift."

"You have read the Bible?" Ellsbeth looked at Erin incredulously.

"Well, yes, parts of it."

"And it says we are saved by faith in Jesus? Surely this cannot be so. Our priest teaches we must earn our way into heaven." Ellsbeth looked at Erin in bewilderment.

They were both startled by the sound of the crossbar sliding and the door opening. The priest Erin had encountered earlier stormed into the room and confronted the girls.

"Ellsbeth! What are you doing here still? When I get my hands on that John, you shall both wish you'd listened better!" He grabbed Ellsbeth roughly by the arm and pushed her toward the door.

"No, wait, please. It's my fault." Erin spoke up in Ellsbeth's defense. "I asked her to stay and talk to me. She wanted to go. I wouldn't let her."

The priest looked askance at Ellsbeth. "You've talked to this girl accused of witchcraft? Tell me what devilment she has whispered in your ear!"

"We just talked. . . ." Ellsbeth said softly. She looked at Erin with fear on her face.

"About what?" the priest demanded.

"Father?"

"Yes?"

"Have you read the Bible?"

"Yes," the priest said haughtily.

"All of it?"

"Well, not every word of it, certainly, but the most important parts." He looked proudly down his nose at the two girls. "And what, may I ask, does that have to do with this discussion?"

"This girl, Erin is her name, has read a part of the Bible that says we are saved by our faith in Jesus, not by the good things we do. Can that be true?" Ellsbeth looked at the cleric with great hope in her eyes.

The priest stood there, looking angrily from one young face to the other. He began to gnash his teeth, and his face turned beet red. With a snarl, he snatched up the little book Erin had dropped from her pocket.

Waving the book in Erin's face, he spoke in low, menacing tones. "You have dared to touch a holy book with your pagan hands?" Then he roared, "The punishment for your deeds can only be death. May God have mercy on your soul." He pushed Ellsbeth, who was now sobbing hysterically, out the door. Before Erin could protest, the door was slammed shut again, and the sound of the bar sliding into place filled the little room.

"Well, Noah," Erin said into the air, "I hope you are having more success than I am."

Suddenly, Erin was very tired. She decided a nap on the straw heap might not be such a bad idea. After carefully setting her glasses on the table, she curled up under her cloak, and drifted off to sleep thinking about Ellsbeth, hoping she was all right.

# 11
# The Peter Principle

FROM SOMEWHERE FAR away, Erin thought she heard her name being called softly, over and over again. She felt so tired, achey, and cold, that opening her eyes seemed like too much of an effort.

She heard her name spoken again. Well, maybe she would open one eye and see who it was. Groaning a little, she rolled over on her side and sat up on one elbow. Opening both eyes, she was pleased to see Noah standing in front of her, several pieces of clothing in his arms.

"Noah!" Erin yawned sleepily. "Where have you been? What time is it?" She sat up, brushing stray pieces of hay off of her clothes and several pieces out of her hair. "You're still in shirt sleeves? In this cold? I can't believe it!" She pulled the cloak around her and shivered.

"To answer your questions in order: I have been walking, running, slipping, and sliding around this village in pursuit of our friend Demont. As to what time it might be, I suggest you either look at your usually reliable wristwatch and judge for yourself as to its possible relevance or accuracy, or listen for the clock chime in the church tower. (Erin glanced at her watch and was unsettled to see it was still 10:37.) And, yes, I'm still in shirt sleeves, but I've brought you more appropriate garb which will hopefully keep you both warmer and less conspicuous." He unceremoniously dumped the load of clothing on top of the still-yawning Erin.

Erin began sorting through the pile of clothing, first to see what was there, and then to see what would fit. Some of the clothing was old and well worn, while other items in the stack looked brand new.

"I suggest that you put these clothes on right over your present apparel. You'll be warmer that way, and we'll not have to carry any surplus with us when we leave."

Erin nodded and began pulling a long, heavy skirt over her bluejeans. She fastened it around her waist with a piece of rope she found in the straw. A beautiful lace-bodiced blouse was too small when pulled over her knit jacket. Searching further, she came up with a plain, off-white shapeless shirt that fit nicely over her head and the jacket. Its sleeves reached to her knuckles, but she thought this could be an advantage once they were out in the cold wind again. As an afterthought, she stuffed the cap on the bottom of the pile into her bluejeans pocket for later use.

"What do you think?" She asked Noah,

whirling around the room, her skirt billowing out around her.

"You will fit in very nicely with the other people here as long as no one looks too closely at you," said Noah approvingly. "I understand you have caused quite a stir amongst the townspeople in the short time you've been shut up here."

"I got a little information from the servant girl who brought me supper. Here, I saved you an apple." Erin handed it to him. "She said we are just outside London, sometime in the 1530s. She wasn't sure about the year." Erin looked at Noah as she readjusted her cloak over her layers of clothing. "I wish I had a mirror. I'll bet my hair is a mess."

"Hmmm . . . the 1530's. London. That was quite an interesting time in earth history, you may recall."

"My research project for school sort of hits close to this time period. In 1492, Columbus was making some significant discoveries. Martin Luther fits in here somewhere, too. I don't know much at all about London in the 1530s. They did have a king, right?"

"Oh, yes, they certainly did: Henry VIII. Are you ready to go?" Noah looked at her expectantly and handed Erin her glasses.

They walked to the bolted door, and Noah

gently pushed against it with the flat of his hand. Erin watched in astonishment as the door swung open just far enough for the two of them to squeeze through. Snow and ice crunched under her sneakered feet. She lifted her skirt so that it didn't drag through the ankle-deep snow.

Looking to her left, she started at the sight of the watchman who was supposed to be keeping guard over her. He seemed to be sleeping standing up, his arms wrapped around himself, a snore coming from his heavily whiskered face.

Noah gently pushed the door shut behind them and gazed up into the night sky. "Look how many stars you can see, Erin," he said softly. "There's no pollution to obscure our view tonight. 'He determines the number of the stars and calls them each by name. Great is our Lord and mighty in power; his understanding has no limit.'"

Erin looked up in delight at the bright spaces in the night sky between the clouds heavy with snow. It was so different from the night sky at home. Home. She felt a sudden stab of homesickness. What were her parents doing? Had Connie called about going to the library? Was Mr. Gather still standing in front of the mirror, wondering where she and Noah were?

"Let's go." Noah walked soundlessly next to Erin whose footsteps crunched loudly and left shallow footprints in the snow.

"Won't the guard hear us?"

"Nope. He probably hasn't slept this well in years," Noah said, grinning.

"Noah," Erin asked suddenly, "why do I get the feeling you've done this before? You seem so calm about all this." She looked at him suspiciously.

Noah didn't answer. He just smiled and looked away. Then Erin heard strains of the "Hallelujah Chorus" from Handel's *Messiah* all around her, and she felt warmed and encouraged.

"The King is in control. We have nothing to worry about."

"Where are we going now?" Erin asked, her sneakers soggy from the snow. "My feet are cold."

"We have to get you out of sight for a while. If there was any doubt that you were a witch before, there will be none after this little escape." Noah led her across the frozen ruts in the road to a path running parallel to them. "But first I want to go back to the place where I left Demont and check on him one more time."

Erin counted as the clock in the church tower chimed.

"Twelve o'clock." Erin's teeth began to chatter. "Are we almost wherever we're going?" Her right hand ached with the cold, and she dropped her skirt. "I'm really getting cold, Noah."

She surprised herself when tears sprang to her eyes. Irrational fear crowded into her mind.

Darkness surrounded them as snow began to fall thicker and faster. Erin struggled to walk in the deepening drifts. Her wet skirt hem gathered bits of snow and ice and unbalanced her. She fell forward suddenly into a deep drift, getting snow in her eyes, nose, and mouth. The urge to cry was stronger than ever.

"Come on, little one," Noah said. "You've walked long enough."

Erin felt herself being lifted up. She was too tired and cold to argue.

As the two travellers moved on into the night, another followed quietly behind, a black dog padding steadily beside him.

The man stopped for a moment, and the dog sat and looked expectantly at his master.

"Well, Tallis, what sayest thou? Be they friends?" The man's English was excellent, but his foreign accent was unmistakable.

The dog raised one paw and gave a short affirmative bark.

"In that case, we'll continue the watch."

Dog and master resumed their quiet tracking.

# 12
# In the Tavern

THROUGH THE SNOW flurries, Erin could see a warm yellow light ahead.

"Think you can walk for a while, Erin?"

"Yes, thanks." Her legs felt wobbly at first, but after a few steps, she found the walking easier. They moved toward the light, and Erin was able to make out a low building ahead of them. The yellow light from inside spilled onto the snow piled haphazardly against its walls.

"That's where I left Demont."

"What is it? Somebody's house?"

"No . . . it's a tavern."

"A tavern!"

"Yes. I'm assuming you know what a tavern is?"

"Well, the only tavern I know about is the one that Indiana Jones visited in *Raiders of the Lost Ark*. Is that the kind of tavern you mean?"

"Yes, as a matter of fact, this one is similar to that one, though probably not as wild . . . or as cold."

"Good." Erin's teeth were chattering again.

"Now, Erin, I'm going to give you two choices. You may stay outside and wait for me to come and get you, which is probably the safer choice, or you may come inside with me and risk being caught a second time."

"I'm too cold and too curious to stay outside," Erin laughed.

"Well, in that case, how fast can you disguise yourself as a boy?"

"Two seconds. The skirt comes off . . . voilá . . . and the hair gets pushed under this cap . . . like so. Instant boy!"

Noah nodded approvingly. "I'm impressed. Let's save the skirt. We'll probably need it later." He rolled it up, tied it like a bedroll with Erin's improvised belt, and gave it to Erin to carry. "Ready for action?"

"Ready."

The pair of travelers crunched to the tavern's worn wooden door, and Noah pushed it open. The noise of laughter and loud talking greeted them along with the smells of food and smoky fires. Two men seated near the door gave them a glance, but no one else seemed to notice them. Noah guided Erin to two seats in a back corner. It felt so good to sit down where it was warm. She slowly leaned her back against the rough plank wall and tried with lowered eyes to scan the faces of the people around her.

"I don't see anyone who even reminds me of Demont." It was difficult to really see in the light created by the oil lamps and the roaring fire in the fireplace. The warmth of the room was so cozy. She could feel herself slipping into sleep, and she had no control over it. The buzz of conversation seemed to be fading away.

Noah's hand on her shirt-sleeve brought her wide awake again. The room was more quiet, but that was because everyone's attention was focused in the same direction. There, standing before the fireplace, was a tall, curly-haired youth talking excitedly to his audience.

Erin sensed a mixed feeling in the crowd. Some of the listeners were genuinely interested in what the boy was saying. But most of them were openly scorning his words, and their interruptions were becoming louder and more frequent.

"I'm telling you," Demont said with fervent conviction, "I can give you the warmth of the sun whenever you want it. You can have fruit and vegetables for your families and bread in abundance all year through."

"Impossible!" shouted one voice.

"Maybe he's responsible for the harsh winter we're having!"

Demont's next words riled the crowd even further. "You are all good men, strong men, capable men. Yet you let another rule you. And this king of yours . . . can he control the seasons of rain or sunshine?"

There was murmuring amongst the men seated around the tables and then a sudden stillness. Demont's face betrayed his panic over the change he sensed in the crowd.

"As your ruler-leader, I promise to be fair and impartial. You will have everything you could possibly want. Just follow me! Follow me!"

There was an explosion of raucous laughter. Demont looked frantically from face to face. He ran from table to table, searching for affirmation, only to be greeted with fresh outbursts of jeers.

"How can he promise control of the seasons? Oh, Noah, I just had a terrible thought. What if he has Dr. Banushta's power panel?" Noah looked at Erin but was kept from comment when a chant started at the tavern keeper's table.

> *Let's throw him out!*
> *Let's throw him out!*
> *Come, join the shout!*
> *Let's throw him out!*

Fists began to beat in time on the tables, and the chant grew louder.

"No! Wait! Listen to me!" Demont tried in vain to gain their attention.

Erin could see the faces of the men sitting at the table closest to the fireplace. She saw two men nod in agreement over what a third said, stand up, and start to walk toward Demont.

"Noah!" She was half out of her own chair when Noah's warning came.

"No, Erin, wait. They won't hurt him."

The room quieted again in anticipation of the coming drama. All eyes were riveted to the two men walking calmly toward Demont. His back was to them at first, but when he sensed their presence, he faced them defiantly.

"James, my friend," said one in a matter-of-fact voice.

"Yes, William, my friend," answered the other.

"Have you heard enough from this young mite who is a bit too full of himself?"

"I certainly have, James."

"Then I have a suggestion, William."

"Yes, James?"

"LET'S THROW HIM OUT!" And with that, the two men grabbed Demont and threw him over William's shoulders like a ten-pound sack of potatoes. Demont started to struggle with only his hands free to punch because William had quite a grip on his legs. James grabbed his fists, much to the approving roar of the crowd, and the two men carried Demont in a kind of parade to all the tables before walking toward the front door. As Demont came closer to Erin, a look of recognition and shocked surprise crossed his face. He started to yell again.

"Witch! Witch! There in the corner!"

William and James only laughed. "Don't try to distract us. You're about to take a little trip, my boy." The two men began to swing Demont back and forth, back and forth, each time his body arched a little higher in the air. Another man opened the front door and bowed in sarcastic respect to the swinging Demont.

"All together, men. That is, all of you who can count to three . . ."

"ONE . . ." the crowd shouted.

"TWO . . ." as Demont swung higher and higher.

"THREE!" They let go of Demont, and he sailed out the door. Erin hoped he landed in one of the snowbanks surrounding the tavern. The crowd cheered and applauded, and James slammed the tavern door.

"I wonder what has created Demont's need for power, for being the one in control?" asked Erin. They watched as the room began to empty, waiting for an opportunity to slip out unobserved. "If he has the panel, then we have all the more reason to return him safely behind the purple door. He could do a lot of damage with that thing."

"To what degree had Dr. Banushta perfected it when you were last with her?" Noah asked Erin.

"Well, she could travel with it, and she was

able to have an effect on the weather behind the purple door."

A stocky man Erin took to be the tavern keeper made his way over to their table. Erin tensed. She had almost forgotten she was a part of the scene in the tavern drama and not an invisible observer.

As the tavern keeper came closer, Erin could see a careworn, wrinkled face, stringy dark hair, and dark eyes. He walked with a noticeable limp, and used the tables and benches to steady himself. He stopped in front of Erin and Noah, his large hands resting flat on the table. He looked hard into Erin's face. Noah seemed to be of no interest to him.

"This is no place for a boy. Get home with you! Push in the bench when you leave since you are the last sitting on it. Good night!" The tavern keeper turned away, reached for the nearest table and continued his closing time rounds.

"Let's go, Erin." Noah rose, and Erin followed. Together they shoved the heavy bench under the table. Once outside, Erin turned to Noah.

"Noah, why is it that no one but I can see you?"

They walked along the path outside the tavern for several steps before Noah answered. "People see what they are capable of seeing."

"That's not an answer, Noah."

"Yes, it is, and it's all the answer I am ready to give now. Come on. Demont is our primary concern at the moment."

Erin gave a grunt of frustration. "Okay, okay. What are we going to do next?"

The clock in the church tower chimed once.

"Given how late . . . or how early it is, depending on your time perspective, I really think we should wait until sun-up to pursue him further."

"I quite agree," a voice broke in. "So, why not come home with me?"

# 13
# Joshua Zayre

TURNING IN SURPRISE, Noah and Erin saw a handsome middle-aged gentleman. His piercing deep-set eyes gazed at them, almost mockingly. He looked directly at Noah and continued, "Come with me. My home is just down this road. We can talk more freely there."

Without waiting for an answer, he turned and began walking rapidly away from them. His heavy cloak billowed around him as the wind picked up. The sleek, energetic black hound trotted alongside him.

"Noah! He saw you!"

"Yes, which can only mean . . . come on, Erin. I'd say our situation is improving!" Noah moved swiftly after the man, the mystified Erin following closely behind him.

Erin couldn't see where they were going through the blur of falling snow. She was glad for the reassurance of Noah's guiding hand on her elbow. She sensed a wall beside her and reached out to touch the rough surface as their guide opened a door in the wall and they passed through. Erin could just make out a rickety staircase now that her eyes had become accustomed to the darkness. It looked dangerous, but again Noah's hand propelled her onward, and she confidently stepped on the bottom step. Their new host was already five steps ahead of her.

"Walk on the side of the step closest to the handrail. Don't step in the middle." He moved quickly up the twisting staircase and waited impatiently for Erin and Noah at the top. He took a large key out of the folds of his cloak and pushed it into the key hole of a heavy, weatherbeaten door.

The spacious room stretched out invitingly before Erin in stark contrast to the dismal outer hall where she now stood. On the floor lay a rich persian rug, warming the room with its deep reds, blues, and beiges. Erin could see a stonehearthed fireplace with a mantel shelf above it.

"Come in, quickly. I don't leave this door open longer than is necessary." Their host hurried them into the room, shutting the heavy door, and pushing two dead bolts into place.

Erin gazed around the room with enormous curiosity. Low shelves on one wall held a number of books. With only the fire giving light to the room, she could barely make out several paintings hanging on the wall opposite the fireplace. Her eyes travelled from frame to frame. Wordlessly, she touched Noah's arm and pointed to the center of the wall.

"Well, what do you know . . ." laughed Noah softly. The firelight reflected back to him from a mirrored surface hanging among the paintings. "Yes, I'd say our situation was definitely improving!" He turned and faced their benefactor.

"We thank you, sir, for bringing us in out of the snow."

The tall man looked at them both with those piercing eyes again. He gave Erin and Noah a knowing look. "You've had quite a night of it, I would say." Erin couldn't identify the accent she heard.

"Señor Joshua Zayre, the King sends His greetings." Noah said to their host.

"You know my name? How is that possible?" The man lost his look of condescension. "Good King Henry sends his greetings only when he wants something, and you two are certainly not among his retinue of servants. You cannot be," he added triumphantly, "because I saw you come into my world in the church sanctuary."

Noah looked at him with calm unconcern. "Shalom, Joshua."

At the sound of the Hebrew word, Joshua Zayre turned pale. "You must never speak thusly

**101**

to me in the hearing of others." His voice fell to a whisper. "Please, who are you? Why have you come?"

Erin looked longingly at the chairs and sofa by the fireplace. She was so tired that even the mystery of this moment wasn't enough to keep her totally conscious. She moved toward the sofa, and the others followed her. Sinking gratefully into the soft cushions, she felt the wonderful relief in her bones that comes after long hours of physical exertion. The man's dog came over to her and thrust his wet nose against her hand, demanding to be petted. She wanted desperately to hear what Noah and this Señor Zayre were saying to each other, but the curtain of sleep came sliding over her, and she willingly let it cover her.

When Erin opened her eyes again, she didn't know where she was. She saw the mantel and wondered how she had managed to fall asleep in Mr. Gather's antique shop. Then, sitting up on one elbow, her eyes took in the rest of the room, and she remembered the events of the night before. Sitting up all the way, she saw Noah standing next to a window, deeply engrossed in a book. He looked up when he heard her stirring.

"Good morning, sleepy head! You're feeling better after your nap, I trust." He closed the book and came and sat beside her.

"What time is it?" Erin asked, still a little groggy.

"Now that is an interesting and complex question. Just what exactly do you mean by 'time?'" he teased. "The watch on your wrist will tell you a time that has no relevancy to where you are at present. The place where you are at present has great relevancy to the time on your watch when considered where that . . ."

"Noah, stop it!" Erin shook him with both hands. "I want facts—plain, simple, logical facts—please, and some food wouldn't hurt either." She stretched and yawned.

A smaller door set in the east wall opened, and Señor Zayre came into the room carrying a tray laden with steaming mugs and a plate stacked with wonderful-looking pastries. "So, the fair maiden has awakened from her long sleep." Zayre put the tray in front of them, offering each a mug.

"Erin, our host, Señor Joshua Zayre, tells me we are in the sixteenth century . . . 1534 to be exact."

"1534 . . . wow!" said Erin under her breath. She looked over at the wall with the paintings. Her eyes came to rest on the beautiful mirror hanging in the center of them. "Señor Zayre, is there anything . . . special . . . about your mirror?"

Joshua Zayre suddenly had a very guilty expression on his face. Not looking Erin or Noah in the eye, he got up. "I do not know, Mistress Erin. I am only keeping what I have been sent. I have more to bring from the kitchen. Excuse me."

# 14
# Clear and Cloudy

"WHAT ABOUT THE mirror, Noah? Is this our way back to Mr. Gather's shop?" Erin got up to look at it more closely. The room was still dark, and now she could hear rain falling. Thunder rumbled suddenly and a flash of lightning brightened all the room's corners for just a second. Erin jumped on seeing her own reflection in the silver glass.

"Oh, do I look a mess!"

The mirror's surface had the same sense of fathomless depth as that of its twin in the twentieth century. The room was too dark to see if the High Council's mark was on the wood. Erin reached out a tentative finger to the smooth, cool-looking surface. She felt the familiar pulling sensation and saw, with no small amount of satisfaction, that her hand was disappearing into the mirror.

"So, it is a companion mirror to ours!" Erin came and sat down next to Noah, combing her long hair with her fingers and rearranging stray wisps of ponytail. "Do you think this one opens into the antique shop?"

"We came through into a church . . . not into

this gentleman's home. Wouldn't it make more sense for the entrances and exits to be in the same place?"

"Noah, why do I get the feeling that you are asking me a question to which you already know the answer?"

"Because you are so perceptive, smarty—a gift of which you will shortly make good use."

Señor Zayre came back into the room, his dog following closely behind. The dog trotted to Erin, sat at her feet, and demanded another head rub.

"Hi, fella. Señor Zayre, what's his name?"

"His name is Tallis."

Upon hearing his name, Tallis wagged his tail, thumping it rhythmically on the edge of the persian rug.

"Tallis, . . ." Erin searched her memory. "Tallis . . . wasn't there a musician named Tallis once?"

Joshua Zayre laughed. "Yes, there certainly *is* . . . I don't think my friend Thomas Tallis would take too kindly to your referring to him in the past tense."

"Sorry," Erin said ruefully. "I keep forgetting where I am . . . which is where again, exactly?"

"You are just outside London, England, January 1534. It is late morning . . . around the eleventh hour, I would guess."

Erin stroked Tallis's head thoughtfully.

"The present king is Henry VIII, the weather both climatologically and politically has been turbulent of late, and life was looking bleak until your arrival."

The rain splattered suddenly against the windowpanes. The room felt colder, and Erin shivered.

"Come, let's bless our repast and eat before the tea gets cold."

They bowed heads, blessed the meal, and Erin and Señor Zayre ate hungrily. Noah kept looking thoughtfully at them both and at the mirror. Tallis walked to each person, giving pleading looks and whines that made Erin laugh.

"What's the matter, Tallis? Are you hungry?"

"He loves bread. *Ven acá*, Tallis, *siéntate*." Tallis obediently sat on his haunches and gobbled down the tossed crust. He licked his chops and got up, begging for more.

The thunder crashed again. The meager light from the fireplace left much of the room shrouded in darkness. Joshua got up from his seat and reached for a candle on the mantle. After lighting it, he began to walk around the room, lighting other strategically placed candlesticks.

"Erin, this wick is too short. Would you please look in that drawer and get a new candle for me?"

Erin pulled open the indicated drawer and gingerly reached into the dark pile of things in search of a new candle. Her fingers touched the waxy surface of a candle stub. As she pulled it free from the layer of papers and assorted articles, a familiar emblem caught her eye. She pulled the drawer out a little further so she could see better.

"Señor Zayre, this paper has the High Council emblem on the corner. Are you a Guardian? Is that why you can see Noah?"

He did not answer her. Wordlessly, he walked over, took the candle stub from her and closed the drawer.

"I have some business in the city. I shall return before nightfall and attend to your needs." He left abruptly, Tallis padding loyally behind him.

"Well. What do you suppose that was all about?" Erin looked at Noah.

"Let's have another look in that drawer." Noah walked over to the little table and pulled open the shallow drawer. He reached inside and pulled out a handful of papers. As he did so, a small object fell to the floor. Erin caught it as it rolled under her chair. It was a ring. A ring with the sign of infinity and a dove flying away in the center . . . a Guardian ring!

"Do you think this belongs to Señor Zayre?

Why would he have the ring of a Guardian and not be wearing it?"

"Well, Erin, remember that your Grandmother De Jong has your grandfather's ring in safe-keeping for you until the Council decides to award it. Perhaps he is keeping it for someone else."

"No, I don't think so. I think the ring is his, and he has taken it off for some reason."

"Not to jump subjects, but where do you suppose our friend Demont has gone?"

"If I know Demont, he's probably holed up somewhere, waiting to go night scavenging again."

"If that is the case, then I suggest you try to sleep a little more, and tonight we'll go after him."

Erin settled down again on the sofa in front

of the fire. She found she was sleepy in spite of the fact that she had slept well into the morning—which was really what time in her century? She closed her eyes and tried to figure it out. She smiled when the sounds of Fauré's *Requiem* floated over her head. She loved that music. "Noah," she said sleepily, "do you realize the *Requiem* score won't be sung for another three hundred years?"

The music stopped momentarily. "Chalk another one up for life in the twentieth century!" Noah said, and then the music began again.

Erin floated along with the beautiful phrases and melodies, at last drifting off into an uneasy sleep. After dreaming about being chased by an angry cleric and falling headlong into a snowbank, Erin awoke, shivering.

"Noah?" she called. "Noah?" she called more urgently. There was no answer. He was gone.

"Noah, I hate it when you do this to me!" Erin hit the sofa cushions in frustration. "He didn't even leave me a note," she grumbled, feeling thoroughly sorry for herself.

Erin sat down in a chair by the window and picked up the book she'd seen Noah reading earlier in the day. It was too dark for her to make out the title. Vowing never to take electricity for granted again, she took the book to the sofa by the fireplace and tried to read it in the dim light of the fire. This book was no stranger to her! It was, in fact, one she knew very well and had dusted on more than one occasion. It was Mr. Gather's Bible.

# 15
# Hold to the Hope

ERIN SAT BACK back on the sofa, Bible in hand. Maybe Noah had gone through the mirror to check its connecting place while she was asleep. Maybe Señor Zayre had already been through the glass and visited the shop and Mr. Gather. Maybe this was an antique Bible from the sixteenth century and Joshua Zayre had owned it first. Well, that would be easy to check. She opened the cover gently and read from the title page. The Bible was the New International Version—definitely a twentieth century accomplishment. That narrowed the possibilities somewhat. As she sat thinking, Tallis streaked into the room from the side door, shaking vigorously, sending a fine spray of droplets into the air. He came over and put a wet head into Erin's lap for some petting.

"Tallis! Please! You're all wet!"

"Tallis! *Ven acá!*" The stern voice called from outside the door. Tallis obediently turned and trotted out the door again, which closed firmly behind him.

Erin got up from her chair and ran to the door. The knob twisted just a little way in her hand and stopped. Locked.

"Okay," she said defiantly into the room at large, "if I'm going to be locked in here, then I am going to explore this room and see what I can find." She turned slowly around the room, trying to decide where she was going to start. The little table with the narrow drawer where she'd found the candle the night before caught her attention. She decided to start there and just keep working her way systematically around the room.

The drawer opened easily, and she slid it out of its wood cabinetry. Settling herself on the rug with the drawer in front of her, Erin began to go through the layers of papers. There were several sheets of music on top of the stack with tunes she tried to hum. The pages under the music turned out to be two letters addressed to Señor Zayre.

"I shouldn't read these. After all, it's rude to read letters meant for other people, even if they are just stuck in a drawer where anyone could find them. And they're probably not even in English." Her self-control enabled her to put the letters next to the sheet music on the rug, but her curiosity led her to peek at the signatures of the senders.

The dim embers in the fireplace gave her just enough light to make out the signatures on both letters Her eyes widened in amazement. Who was this Joshua Zayre, anyway? Why would he have letters from Christopher Columbus, of all people? Boy, would these make great visual aids for her research project!

Eagerly she reached into the drawer's shallow depths. Her fingernails scraped against the wooden bottom as her fingers wrapped around the last of the papers in the drawer. She gently pulled the rolled sheaf of papers out, looked into the drawer again, and saw the Guardian ring rocking gently in one corner. She added that to her mystery pile and sat down on the carpet to investigate the last documents.

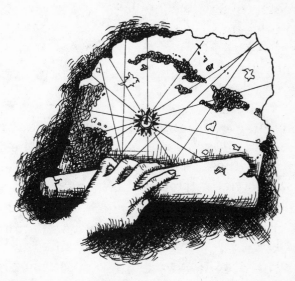

The rolls of parchment wouldn't stay unrolled long enough for Erin to study them. She only got enough of a glimpse to recognize configurations somewhat familiar to her—these had to be maps. She needed something heavy to weigh down the corners. Taking the Bible, scrolls, papers, and ring over to the table by the window, she pulled four books off the shelf next to it. After a couple of awkward minutes of struggle, she finally sat back to study the now secured work before her.

"See, here, girl! What are you doing?"

Erin had been so involved in her discoveries that she hadn't heard anyone come into the room.

"Well, when you locked me in, I . . . sort of went exploring." she stammered.

To her relief, Joshua Zayre laughed. "Exploring in this room? And what treasures have we found?" He walked over to Erin's treasure pile on the table and lit a small lamp.

"Señor Zayre, did you know Christopher Columbus? I didn't read your letters, but I couldn't help seeing the signature on the last pages. And these maps. . . ." Erin stopped. Over and above her curiosity she sensed pain and sorrow coming from Señor Zayre. She had never before sensed emotion coming from another so tangibly. She was shaken and mystified by this new perception. "I'm sorry if I've upset you. Here, I'll put these things away." Erin picked up two of the books holding down the corners of the map and watched it snap shut.

**116**

Joshua Zayre wordlessly stood by as Erin neatly restacked the papers and returned them to the drawer. She went back to retrieve the ring, and was surprised to find it gone.

"Señor Zayre, I had the Guardian ring here, too. Now where did? . . ."

Zayre held the ring up for her to see and then dropped it in his pocket.

Erin pushed the little drawer back into the chest and smiled when bouncing Baroque melodies burst into the room. Noah was back.

"Why does music seem to follow you, Señor Sebastian? Is it through some twentieth-century musical magic?"

"Noah just thinks about music and it spills over into the atmosphere," Erin explained. "Noah, where have you been? Have you located Demont again? What are we going to do next?"

Noah looked at the two of them thoughtfully. "Yes, I have located Demont, and we will go after him shortly. But first, Señor Joshua Zayre, why is the Guardian ring in your pocket and not on your finger? Is it not yours to wear?"

Erin felt the waves of Joshua's pain and sorrow wash over her again. Across her mind's eye there galloped sudden flashes of pictures: A rolling ship, people yelling in a language she didn't understand, a beautiful blue-green lagoon, a young woman holding a baby and calling out a

**117**

name Erin recognized—Joshua!

Noah looked at her expectantly. Joshua Zayre looked out the window into the greyness, saying nothing.

Had her imagination run away with her as it did so often, or did what she was sensing and seeing about Señor Zayre have meaning? How could she find out without seeming silly . . . or crazy?

Joshua turned and faced them both. "The Guardian ring is mine. It was my father's before me, though I don't think he was ever the wearer of it, only the keeper. I have taken it off because I. . . ." He stopped, and Erin felt again his sweeping sorrow. "I do not wear the ring now because I have lost my ability to hold to the hope of my guardianship."

*Hold to the hope.* Erin thought about those words. She wondered what she would do if she ever came to the place where she could no longer hold to the hope.

Joshua Zayre looked out the window and spoke softly, more to himself than to them. "Life held so much for me once. As a young lad of twelve, I was assigned to the ship of Admiral Christopher Columbus. He and my father were friends. I had no idea at the time that my life was in danger, and that was why I was sent so far from home on a perilous voyage. I only saw the beckoning finger of lady adventure."

Erin racked her brain for the research she had done on Christopher Columbus. "Are you Spanish, then?"

"Yes, though I have not seen my homeland in over forty years."

Erin saw again the storm, heard the people yelling, and smelled the fresh air of the blue-green lagoon.

"We set sail in the year of our Lord, 1492."

"You must have been one of the boys on board Columbus's ship that I read about. Your parents must have been proud to have their son on such an historic voyage." Then Erin wondered if Joshua had any idea of the significance of his part in world history.

**119**

"I don't know how they felt."

"I don't understand."

"When we returned in 1493, my family was gone. I never found them again."

"Gone?" Erin asked incredulously. "Didn't they leave word where they went so you could join them? An address? A phone num . . ." she stopped herself, remembering her present century.

"The Spanish Inquisition was in full bloom. King Ferdinand and Queen Isabella expelled all Jews from Spain in 1492. I learned they had been deported the same day we set sail from Cadiz. They did not dare leave any knowledge of their whereabouts. Admiral Columbus felt responsible for me and arranged safe passage for me out of the country. I have been a vagabond with numerous hats and disguises these many years." Joshua Zayre's dark eyes burned with a sudden anger.

"How have you managed to establish yourself with the King of England if your roots are Spanish? I didn't think England had any relations with Spain during this century."

"Occasionally I am a source of funds for the king."

Zayre walked over to the bookshelf and took down a nine-pronged candle holder. He set it on the table before them. It looked old to Erin.

There were letters in Hebrew on the sides of the pedestal that supported the nine candle cups. Erin recognized several of the Hebrew characters. Her father sang at temple for the Jewish High Holy Days and had shown Erin the interesting letters.

"When I returned and found my family gone, I ran through the house, searching every room for some sign of them. There was nothing. All of their possessions were gone. But there was one place only I would know to look: our secret hiding place. I found this menorah there."

"It's beautiful, but that doesn't explain about the money."

Wordlessly, Joshua picked up the menorah

and turned it upside down. He unscrewed the base, revealing a hollow compartment.

"Don't tell me, let me guess," said Erin excitedly. "That was a hiding place for something—diamonds or rubies!"

Zayre nodded. He replaced the bottom and set the menorah back on the table. "Yes, there was a lifetime of wealth in that little menorah along with the Guardian ring, but I would trade it all to know what happened to my parents."

"And the baby?" asked Erin without thinking.

Joshua turned to her sharply. "How did you know about the baby? No, don't tell me. I don't want to know any more." Fumbling in his pocket, he pulled out the Guardian ring and tossed it to Noah. "Take it back to High Council. It is theirs now, not mine. When as a young man I was offered the guardianship of my forefathers, that of being the guardian of ideas and visions, I accepted with great delight. For more than twenty years I have watched visions and ideas born into this world, and I have watched them die, destroyed on the Inquisition racks and burned on the bonfires of town squares."

"But Señor Zayre, where we are in my century has everything to do with what you have done in yours—and things have turned out amazingly. I live in a country where people are

**122**

free to worship, think, and speak as they please."

"Where is this place? I would like to go there."

"You've been very close already."

Zayre shook his head in disbelief, strode across the room and went to the side door.

"Señor Zayre, you are looking in the wrong direction for your hope," Noah said. "People will always disappoint you at one time or another. Look up. Look to God. He is your source of hope."

Face taut with emotion, Señor Zayre left Erin and Noah alone in the room.

"He speaks more from his own disappointment and pain than from what is really happening in this century," Noah said softly.

Erin was silent. It was painful and frustrating for her to witness so much distress in another. What was the good in knowing someone else was hurting if you didn't know how to help?

# 16
# Unexpected Motivation

"TO BRING US back to the task at hand, I have found Demont close by," said Noah. "He's sharing a shelter with three hogs and a cow and is not at all happy, which will certainly work to our benefit."

"How do you propose we get him to talk to us, let alone come with us through this mirror? This *is* the way back, isn't it?"

Noah laughed. "Yes, it's the way back." He looked in the direction of Mr. Gather's Bible. "I see you found the same clue I did. I have a feeling that very soon Señor Zayre will be confessing to a visit to the twentieth century."

"Noah, I feel so sad for him. I can't imagine how it must feel to have lost hope. I wish there was a way to show him the future, so he would know how important his guardianship is, and how much of an effect this century had on the future. If he could just sit down with Mr. Gather and talk, I know he'd feel better."

"Maybe you will have a chance to talk to him before we leave. Right now I want to get Demont in here and have a little chat with him."

"Noah, there's something else I need to talk to you about—something that's happening to me."

Señor Zayre's reentry silenced her. He had a large cloth sack in one hand and a stout piece of twine in the other. "Will this hold the boy?"

"Yes, that should do very nicely. This will only take a few minutes, Erin. It will be safer for you to stay here and wait for us."

"Oh, no, you aren't leaving me here again, are you? I haven't gotten to do anything on this trip except stay where I'm told. I want to come, please, Noah?"

"We will be right back, I promise. And if anyone saw you, it would be bad for Señor Zayre. You don't want to cause him any more trouble, do you?"

Erin shook her head. Angry and frustrated, she watched them go out the door, then stomped across the room and bounced down hard on the couch, crossing her arms.

Before she had a chance to settle comfortably into her black mood, the door reopened, admitting a triumphant Joshua and Noah, firmly grasping the now lumpy, squirming sack which had been tied shut with the twine.

"Let . . . me . . . out!" a familiar voice shouted from inside the sack.

"All right! You got him!" said Erin gleefully. She watched as the two men gently set the squirming bundle on the hardwood floor and tried to untie the knotted cord.

"Demont," yelled Zayre, "you'll have to hold still so I can untie this rope."

"You're both kidnappers! I'm telling! Let . . . me . . . out!" The sack rolled dangerously close to the fire.

Between the two men, the knot was undone. They stood back and let Demont wiggle his way out. Señor Zayre had locked the front door and slid the deadbolts in place. He and Noah blocked the side door, ready for Demont's escape attempts.

Free of the sack, Demont angrily looked from one face to another. He ran to the front door and rattled the door knob. Then he turned and tried to butt his way through to the side door, but Señor Zayre just caught him by the waist and swung him onto the couch. Demont tried the butting tactic five times before he stopped. Then he held his head in his hands and started to cry in frustration.

Noah motioned Erin to begin talking to Demont. Erin walked a few steps forward and spoke his name softly, "Demont?"

He didn't look up.

"Demont, we're here to help you. This isn't a safe time or place for you. Please come back with Noah and me."

Erin took another step toward Demont and was rewarded for her concern with a swift kick in the ankle.

"Stay away from me, Erin-sneak. I won't go back there. I won't. I know what you are really after, and I won't give it back. Dr. Banushta dropped it. Finders keepers."

Erin knew he was talking about the power panel.

"Demont, the girl is right. This century isn't safe for the likes of you. Go back with them before my fellow countrymen catch you and burn you at the stake for witchcraft . . . or whatever else they decide is appropriate."

Demont looked at Joshua Zayre warily. He shifted his weight on the couch. He looked tired and afraid, almost like Arnold Lorenzo, Erin thought irrelevantly.

"Demont, how old are you?"

"I . . . I . . . don't know," he said softly.

"When is your birthday?" Upon asking that question, Erin felt great emotion coming from Demont, a combination of anger and hate in his expression.

"My day of birth was not recorded, remembered, or ever told to me. It was not considered important enough. I . . . I . . . was not considered important enough." He emphasized his words by hitting his fists on the arm of the couch.

"Oh, Demont, I'm sorry. That's awful . . . of course you are important! How could anyone think otherwise?"

Erin took yet another step toward the boy. She could easily have reached out and touched his bowed head, but she didn't, remembering his aversion to physical contact.

"We think you are important—important enough to come after. We are concerned for your safety, Demont. You might get hurt. Please come home with us. . . ."

The room filled with the sobs of the boy. He rested his forehead on his knees and rocked back and forth. "I have . . . no . . . home." He looked up at Erin with a bewildered expression, all the craftiness gone from his tear-streaked face. "You really came after me because you thought I might get hurt?"

Erin sat down opposite him on the couch. She left plenty of room between herself and Demont. "Yes. Noah and I have been specially sent to find you. Please come with us."

"No one listens to me here. It's even worse than behind the purple door." Demont looked with renewed helplessness at Erin.

The intensity of the moment was broken by wild pounding on Zayre's front door.

"Señor Joshua? Señor Joshua! Please open the door! It's Ellsbeth! Please!"

Zayre unlocked and unbolted the front door, let the caller in, and quickly locked it behind her again. The young girl didn't even look at the other occupants of the room, she only had eyes for Joshua.

"They are burning things . . . books . . . in the square . . . it's awful . . . please . . . you have to get away!" The girl was frantic and gripped Joshua's arm ferociously. "They said they were coming here next. Señor Joshua hurry . . . get away . . . they will hurt you . . . or kill you!"

"Ellsbeth, you're not making sense. Tell me from the beginning what is happening."

Ellsbeth took a deep breath and turned. She gasped when she saw Erin and Demont. "You!" she exclaimed. She turned again to Zayre, confusion and concern on her face. "If they are found here, all will be lost."

"Ellsbeth," persisted Joshua, "who is burning what?"

"A group of men is burning books in the town square. I heard one of them say they were coming here next—they know that you have a collection of books, and they plan to burn them, too."

Joshua turned away from the girl toward his books. He shook his head slowly, then turned and faced them with a look of resignation. "Ellsbeth, out the back way with you now, there's a good girl." He shoved the frightened servant girl out the side door and closed it behind her. Then he stepped purposefully over to the bookshelves and ran his hand across several volumes, pulling three off the shelf, handing them to Erin.

"Here, Erin. Take these back to your time. And take this, too," he handed her the menorah. She grasped the load tightly.

They could now hear angry shouts from the entrance to Zayre's rooms. Tallis started barking, running to the door, half leaping at it.

"Time to go, Demont, Erin." Noah spoke almost matter-of-factly.

"Noah! We can't leave Señor Zayre to face this alone! Can't we do something? Can't *you* do something?"

The shouts grew louder, and Erin was horrified to hear the sound of splintering wood. They must have axed their way into the hallway. It would be only a matter of seconds before the ax was laid to the door leading into this room. She only hoped the look of the rickety stairway discouraged them from coming up too quickly.

Erin, Noah, Demont, and Joshua waited breathlessly for the next sounds to come. Surprisingly, all was quiet. Erin turned and looked questioningly at Noah. Then the unspoken question was answered. She smelled the strong odor of wood smoke. The intruders must have set fire to the stairway!

Demont smelled it, too. "We must go! Fire! I'll go back with you to the purple door. Let's go.

Now!" He ran to the mirror. Erin watched with relief as he leaped through. She only hoped Mr. Gather was on the other side, ready to steer Demont back through the purple door.

# 17
# Home Again

SMOKE POURED UNDER the door and began to fill the room. Erin felt her eyes water, and an overpowering tickle rose in her throat.

"Erin, go through the mirror. I'll follow after we've finished here."

Erin ran over to the mirror and gently tossed the books Joshua had given her through the glass. The menorah she held in one hand and grabbed hold of Tallis's collar with the other. He walked with her as far as the mirror and stopped.

"Come on, Tallis. Come on, boy. We have to leave now."

The dog twisted and pulled. He was strong, and Erin felt her grip loosening. The smoke in the room was very thick now, and little fingers of flame were reaching into the room under the bottom of the door.

"Joshua, they are waiting for you outside." said Noah. "Is there another way out besides the way you sent Ellsbeth?"

"Yes," Joshua smiled grimly. "The wise man always has more than one way of escape." He ran over to the window and opened it. Straddling the sill, he turned back to Noah, Erin, and Tallis. "My neighbor's courtyard lies below."

"Joshua, wait. Aren't you forgetting something?" Noah held up the Guardian ring.

Joshua hesitated for only a second before extending his open hand toward Noah. Noah tossed the ring through the air. Señor Zayre caught it, and grinning broadly, he slid it back on his finger. "God go with you," he said and disappeared from view.

Tallis broke free of Erin's hold and bounded out the window after him.

"Oh, no! Tallis! Come back!"

"Tallis has enough sense to know where he belongs. Let's go, Erin. It's getting a little warm in here."

Erin held the menorah with both hands and leaped through the mirror, hoping for a soft landing on the other side. She landed feet first on the familiar floor of Antiques, Antiquities, Inc., the three books scattered on the carpet in front of her.

"Mr. Gather?" The front door stood ajar.

Mr. Gather came back in upon hearing his name. "Erin! Demont just came through the mirror and ran out the front door. Parenthesis managed to trip him, but it only slowed him down. He's already run across the field . . . and where is Mr. Sebastian?"

**134**

"Mr. Gather, there was a fire. That's what motivated Demont to come back through the mirror. Noah was right behind me."

They both turned to face the silver glass. Its surface seemed to be glowing a soft red, then orange, then deep, deep blue. Erin could see flames licking around the edges of the mirror's frame.

"He won't be able to come back if this is destroyed, will he?"

"Oh, I wouldn't worry yet," Mr. Gather said calmly. "A wise man always has more than one way of escape." He smiled at Erin.

With a suddenness that startled them both, Noah Sebastian bounded through the mirror and into the room. He landed neatly on his feet, his face covered with soot, the smell of smoke clinging to his clothing. He had Mr. Gather's Bible in his hand.

The mirror glass shattered, the frame burned as though made of paper, and burning coals dropped onto the carpet, then disappeared.

"Noah! I thought you were right behind me."

"I just wanted to make sure that Señor Zayre and Tallis were well on their way before the book burners discovered they had escaped." He bent down and picked up the three books Joshua had given Erin. "Señor Zayre sent these to you, Mr. Gather." He handed Mr. Gather two of the beautifully bound volumes.

"Oh, my. These are wonderful! *Canterbury Tales* and *Cosmographiae Introductio* . . . both unique testimonies to times long past." Mr. Gather sat down, eager to study the books more carefully.

"And this one is for you, I think, Erin." Noah handed her a smaller, cloth-covered volume.

Mystified, Erin took it out of his hands. "It's Señor Zayre's diary! Wow! But, Noah, it's not in English. I guess that's one way to keep your diary from being read by others: write it in a foreign language! I'll have to learn Spanish now."

"Erin, where is Demont?"

Demont. They had momentarily forgotten about Demont.

"Well, he is here, isn't he?" asked Noah.

"Oh, yes. He's here all right. Here in the twentieth century . . . in possession of Dr. Banushta's power panel."

"Oh, no!"

"Hello, everyone!" came a new voice. "Erin! Where did you get those neat clothes?" Connie walked into the shop. "I'm here to get my mom's birthday present, Mr. Gather. How much do you want for the angel you have on top of the apothecary cabinet?" Connie's eagle eye fell on the rumpled Noah. "Wow, Mr. Sebastian! Rough day at work?"

**136**

"You could say that," he grinned.

Erin had so many unanswered questions. She watched as Mr. Gather took down the angel from the top of the cabinet and set it on his desk for Connie. She felt a hand on her shoulder and looked up into Noah's blackened face.

"Señor Zayre and Tallis got away all right?" she asked softly.

"Yes, they certainly did."

"I'm glad. But I wish we could have helped him and encouraged him more. To have lost hold of your hope, that must be awful."

"We have lost hold of Demont. I'd better go find him. . . ." Noah went out of the shop's front door.

Erin sat down thoughtfully in her chair, Señor Zayre's diary in hand, and was pleasantly surprised by Parenthesis jumping into her lap. The cat sniffed Erin's hands and meowed accusingly as if to say, "You've been petting another animal!" As Erin stroked the cat's silky head, her eyes fell on her fingers.

"Well, Parenthesis, Señor Zayre took his ring off and put it on again . . . and I have yet to put my ring on for the first time. High Council certainly does take its time giving out commendations." She put the cat down on the rug and stood up. "Mr. Gather, has Connie talked you into a good price for that angel yet?"

# Epilogue

"It's about time you got here!" a voice whispered good-naturedly to Noah. "I've been standing in this poison ivy for at least five minutes!"

Noah scooted behind the tree with the other angel. "Hi, Sam. I knew I could depend on you to find Demont for me."

"Man, where have you been? You're filthy!"

"Thanks a lot. I've been chasing our friend here."

Both angels looked into the backyard where Demont was hiding. He was crouched behind the compost pile at the far end of a brick patio.

"Getting him back behind the purple door should be fairly easy between the two of us."

"I wouldn't be so sure of that if I were you. I've already chased him across four centuries. . . ."

"You know, Noah, he doesn't look so good. Are you sure he's not sick or something?"

"Think about how you'd look if you were hiding behind that pile of garbage." But Noah looked at Demont with new concern. Sam was right. Demont didn't look well at all.

Suddenly, both angels tensed. Demont stood up, gave a loud cry, and fainted. The back door of the house flew open, and Arnold Lorenzo and his mother came running onto the patio.

"I think things just got a lot more complicated," said Sam.

"Yes . . ." Noah replied with a frown. "I think a certain young lady will earn her Guardian ring before this is over."